PENGUIN BOOKS

WATCH YOUR LANGUAGE

Terrance Hayes is the author of *American Sonnets for My Past and Future Assassin*, winner of the 2019 Hurston/Wright Legacy Award, and *Lighthead*, winner of the 2010 National Book Award. His other poetry collections are *So to Speak*, *How to Be Drawn*, *Wind in a Box*, *Hip Logic*, and *Muscular Music*. He is also the author of *To Float in the Space Between: A Life and Work in Conversation with the Life and Work of Etheridge Knight*, winner of the 2019 Poetry Foundation Pegasus Award for Poetry Criticism. His honors include a National Endowment for the Arts Fellowship, a Guggenheim Fellowship, and a 2014 MacArthur Fellowship. Hayes lives in New York City, where he is a professor of creative writing at New York University.

Also by Terrance Hayes

POETRY
So to Speak
American Sonnets for My Past and Future Assassin
How to Be Drawn
Lighthead
Wind in a Box
Hip Logic
Muscular Music

NONFICTION
To Float in the Space Between: A Life and Work in Conversation with the Life and Work of Etheridge Knight

WATCH YOUR LANGUAGE

**Visual and Literary Reflections on a
Century of American Poetry**

Terrance Hayes

 **PENGUIN BOOKS**

PENGUIN BOOKS
An imprint of Penguin Random House LLC
penguinrandomhouse.com

LIBRARY OF CONGRESS CATALOGING-IN-PUBLICATION DATA
Names: Hayes, Terrance, author.
Title: Watch your language : visual and literary reflections on a century
  of American poetry / Terrance Hayes.
Description: [New York] : Penguin Books, [2023]
Identifiers: LCCN 2022059877 (print) | LCCN 2022059878 (ebook) |
  ISBN 9780143137733 (paperback) | ISBN 9780593511855 (ebook)
Subjects: LCSH: American poetry—20th century—History and criticism. |
  Poetics. | LCGFT: Literary criticism. | Creative nonfiction.
Classification: LCC PS323.5 .H33 2023 (print) |
  LCC PS323.5 (ebook) | DDC 811/.509—dc23/eng/20221003
LC record available at https://lccn.loc.gov/2022059877
LC ebook record available at https://lccn.loc.gov/2022059878

Printed in the United States of America
1st Printing

Set in Berling LT Std with Neue Plak
Designed by Sabrina Bowers

for my parents & teachers

I want to draw a map, so to speak, of a critical geography and use that map to open as much space for discovery, intellectual adventure, and close exploration . . .

TONI MORRISON, *PLAYING IN THE DARK*

Contents

Preface:
How to Use This Book

Reading is a mix of telepathy and time travel. It's a magical transference of information, knowledge, and mystery: the context, text, and subtext of a reader's life. I consider my life evidence. My life is made possible because of my writing, but my writing is made possible because of my reading. Does reading require talent? No, reading requires stamina and time—two things that may yield the same fruit as talent. Reading poetry is an especially refined kind of telepathy, says a poetry enthusiast. A life teaching poetry has meant a life teaching the magic in reading and reading to write. Every reader is a potential writer. I don't say every good or bad reader is a good or bad writer. Such judgments don't matter when the act of reading is, like the act of writing, mostly a matter of keeping an eye on your thinking, of bearing witness, of keeping record. Drawing, which, for me, is close to the act of writing, is also a way to watch your language.

I learned to write in the public libraries of Columbia, South Carolina. I learned to write in Coker College's library and later the library of the University of Pittsburgh. I found a poem by Yusef Komunyakaa in one of those libraries and poems by Toi Derricotte in another. That I later found those two poets in the world is my particular good fortune. This book is dedicated to Derricotte and Komunyakaa, and to the many poets I read *to know*. *Watch Your Language* maps a landscape of literary, cultural, and personal influence. Toni Morrison's quote from the opening chapter of her book *Playing in the Dark* contextualizes this collection as well as my new poetry collection, *So to Speak*.

> I want to draw a map, so to speak, of a critical geography and use that map to open as much space for discovery, intellectual adventure, and close exploration . . .

Where the poems map poetic forms and expressions, this prose collection maps poetic reading and interpretation. The sections of *So to Speak* ("Watch Your Mouth," "Watch Your Step: The Kafka Virus," and "Watch Your Head") are in conversation with the range of visual and textual explorations throughout *Watch Your Language*. A medley of essays, inventive formations of book reviews, and biographical prose poems appear amid a mercurial poetry time of questions divided into nine musing sections across the collection. Question 1: "If you decided to chart your genealogy according to the poets and poetry you know, would it be more comprehensive than what you know of your actual family?" Question 186: "If you don't see suffering's potential as art, will it remain suffering?" Like any guidebook, this book should leave the curious reader with more questions than answers. A theory of American poetry becomes a practice of inquiry and invention.

Watch Your Language offers the names and details of the known and less known poets housed in the mind, heart, and library of a poetry enthusiast. Any book that matters to a reader is literature. Any book that matters to a reader is permanently housed in their mental, emotional, psychic library. It is the sort of library Italo Calvino describes in *The Uses of Literature*. He imagines a culture's most significant books at the center of an ever-expanding, borderless library: "Literature is a search for the book hidden in the distance that alters the value and meaning of the known books; it is the pull toward the new apocryphal text still to be rediscovered or invented." I hope any reader convinced of this constructs the appropriate fluid, personal genealogy of reading; a creative shelter, a psychic data bank, a resource for living. *Watch Your Language* offers a model for watching language wherever you find it.

My first prose book, *To Float in the Space Between*, engaged a single poet and poem. In the *New York Times* Ed Pavlic wrote, "The question of influence becomes one of connection more than resistance, collaboration more than anxiety. Hayes reminds us that the word 'influence' is at root fluid." In the National Book Critics Circle Citation for *To Float in the Space Between*, Walton Muyumba wrote, "Working in a kind of essayistic confessional style, Hayes considers political poetry, black masculinity, the end of marriage, absent biological fathers, the affections that fathers hold for sons, the beginning of love, kinship, and dream song." *Watch Your Language* expands scope to reflect on over a century of poets and poetry, on both canonized and overlooked poets. Like all views of history, the history of American poetry is full of blind spots and wormholes.

I shudder at all that's covered by my blind spots, biases, and limitations. I can never say enough—I will have to write more about my bond to the poets of my generation, to my peers and students who have become peers, to my spirit sister, Elizabeth Alexander, and my bond beyond words to Yona Harvey. The bonds of your influence are boundless.

Toni Morrison, James Baldwin, Gwendolyn Brooks, Toi Derricotte, Yusef Komunyakaa—essentially every poet mentioned (and several forgotten) in these pages has impacted my outlook on poetry. I could not have completed this book without the teachers I found in books. Christopher MacGowan's guide and reference book, *Twentieth-Century American Poetry*, has been foundational in my survey of poetry courses for more than twenty years, and was an invaluable resource in the construction of my poetry timeline and this preface, for example. I express my gratitude to Christopher MacGowan and the makers of the Blackwell Guides to Literature series for supporting teachers, writers, and readers. My prose style plays across a pastiche of genres and tones. I aim paradoxically for Michael Schmidt's clarity and thoroughness in the nonfiction biographical sketches of *Lives of the Poets* and Roberto Bolaño's discursiveness and mischief in the mock biographies of *Nazi Literature in the Americas*. In his preface to *Memory of Fire*, Eduardo Galeano says his approach to writing about history was antithetical to the way he'd learned history in school:

> History classes were like visits to the waxworks or the Region of the Dead. The past was lifeless, hollow, dumb. They taught us about the past so that we should resign ourselves with drained consciences to the present: not to make history, which was already made, but to accept it.

Memory of Fire is another central book in the conception of this text. *Watch Your Language* muses over a century or so of American poetry with Galeano's attitude and lyric documentary view. It is the gaze of someone daydreaming through history; someone skipping English class to wander the aisles of the library. I admit an interest in poems produced after the Great Migration, around the birth of Gwendolyn Brooks in 1917. I am interested in a history of American poetry adjacent to Brooks and those influenced by Brooks in the last century. Even Christopher MacGowan's comprehensive text omits work by Gwendolyn Brooks from its list of seminal poetry collections of the twentieth century. *Watch Your Language* investigates, revises, and reinvents the presences and omissions of a shared poetic history.

In the "How to Use This Book" section of *Twentieth-Century American Poetry*, MacGowan writes that his chronology "sets out the major social, political, and literary events of the century as they provide a broad context for the poetry." Poetry speaks across time and space. Your library is a time-traveling machine. This collection may be used as a guide or reference in creating your own poetic journey.

Terrance Hayes, October 2022

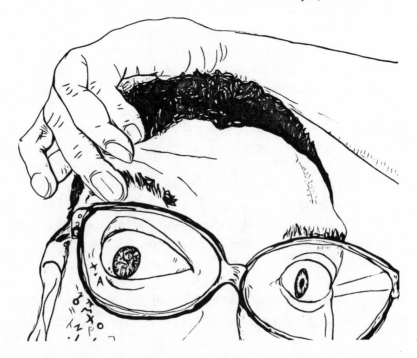

WATCH YOUR LANGUAGE

Between Practice, 1984

1. Afternoons in Florida while my favorite, jocular cousin suffered summer school, I climbed the tall, hot fence of the elementary school behind his house to practice and dream of dunks. **2.** I was thirteen, my mother was on a Caribbean cruise ship in a state of longing, her husband was on a German army base in a state of longing; they left me with relatives in a distant state. **3.** Sometimes I talked with the posters on my cousin's walls: robed Moses Malone dividing a sea of basketballs, George "Iceman" Gervin, sitting with his long legs crossed on an ice throne as he palmed two silver basketball spheres with a cool I tried carrying with me out to the basketball court where the heat stretched my bones. **4.** Sometimes my cousin Noonpie would stand at the fence and after a moment or two call me in to the terrible boredom of a house packed with her four other sisters. Once the two oldest girls pinned me to the floor, the oldest sister straddling me while the strongest sister held my face and covered my panic in lipstick. I recall it now, my made-up face in the mirror, with pleasure. **5.** I have said so little about poetry because I knew so little about poetry then. **6.** Mute, fluid, confused, determined, sometimes Noonpie and I dry-humped in a large walk-in closet. She was my age. Sometimes she leafed through my drawing book. Once my cousin, aka her older brother, found us and yanked me by my ankles into the air, upside down and flailing like a fish pulled from a bucket of water. **7.** I may have known by way of intuition the silences that come before poetry: our silence when a relative named TinPan appeared on the doorsteps one night with a knife wound's evidence staining his shirt and the woman of the house led him to her bathroom; our silence when the day after a Black boy was covered suddenly, permanently, by the lake near their home; the mute, fluid, confused, determined practice of silence, the practitioners of silence. **8.** Noonpie and her siblings knew they were not my blood cousins because their parents told them, but I was loved with the severity and indifference and kindness any cousin receives. **9.** I spent some afternoons studying old photos of the man of the house: a tall, very black man. In them he wore a basketball uniform and looked more like one of his daughters than his son. I took him as proof basketball was in my blood, because I did not know then that we were not blood. **10.** The woman of the house was my stepfather's aunt. Her tongue often cut everything and everyone down to size. **11.** My mother was afraid of her. **12.** Once when my cousin took me to play basketball, we stood first with his friends beneath a few trees and smoked weed. Though I only got one puff, it ruined me for the game. I would have been ruinous even without the dope, to be honest. "Man, if I had that nigga height," laughed one of my cousin's friends. I was wasted, I was a waste. **13.** Because it was a small, mostly Black beach town at the edge of a big, mostly white beach town, the teenage Black boys tried harder to be hard. Some of them jumped tourists, taking their money, beach gear, and sunglasses. Some of them vanished quickly into jails or shotgun houses full of drugs and broken women. My cousin survived on charm and luck. His sisters survived because they remained locked in their father's house. **14.** "Do you want to be a basketball player?" the man of the house asked me when he found me holding his son's basketball in my lap. "Do you want to be an artist?" he asked me when I showed him my notebook drawings. "Do you want to be a man?" the man of the house asked me when he found me weeping because my mother had not returned. **15.** He's going to be seven feet tall, my cousin bragged when his friends asked my age. I was thirteen and already more than six feet high. **16.** I'd look at the man of the house looking at the photos of himself as a young basketball player. I'd listen to the way he talked to his son at dinner. I was there when his wife smoked cigarettes, lacing profanity through the affections she shared with him. Her death, years later, would be the reason for his death shortly thereafter. **17.** You must be a foot taller, my mother said when she finally returned, but to me, it was she who seemed smaller. **18.** After my cousin told me strong calf muscles were the secret to jumping power, I set the balls of my feet at the edge of the stairs in the house, lowering my heels as far as I could toward the floor, then pressing my heels up as high as I could for as many times as I could as often as I could. **19.** "My mother's relatives are tall," I told the boys in Florida when they asked where I'd gotten my height. "My father's relatives are tall," I told the boys back home when they asked where I'd gotten my height. **20.** I used to think practice was preparation for the game, but now I believe the game is what happens between practice. **21.** What I remember is the way the man of the house looked over my drawings. Snoopy's nose needed to be longer, he said. Why did the people only have three fingers? he asked. Then he'd push the pages back to me and say he wanted to see improvements tomorrow. **22.** Again and again the ball jammed against the front of the rim, jolting my whole body backward and back to the tarmac. Or the ball ricocheted from the rim, arcing overhead. Sometimes I'd glance toward the fence, relieved Noonpie was not there watching, when I jogged to retrieve the basketball. **23.** I failed so often I came to accept it was failure I was practicing. In poetry I have failed so often I have come to accept it is failure I am practicing. **24.** My stepfather's mother had him when she was fourteen. She was barely around those summers. My stepfather knew almost nothing about his father and did not care to ask. He was raised by a man named "Stick," but if you ask him he will say he raised himself. **25.** I should not call him my stepfather. I have never called him my stepfather. **26.** First the mother died and shortly thereafter the man of the house died. And later my father's mother died. My father wept and I was angry to see him weeping. Though Florida was his home, he was rarely there those summers. **27.** We have never discussed our fathers or mothers, though the space between our fathers and mothers is what makes us like one another. **28.** The first time I dunked that summer no one was there to see it. Not even I was witness. The ball passed suddenly through the rim, and though I had been trying for weeks, I did not know how it happened when it happened. I tried again and again to do it again.

Reflections and Foresight upon a Century of Poetry, 2016

All the highlights of my first day in Shanghai my first time in China featured Guan Guan, an eighty-eight-year-old Taiwanese poet who said he did not write poems. It might have been mistranslated to me in the ruckus of the first, and I think last, Shanghai International Poetry Festival. There was a famous American Pulitzer poet, an old English poet, a young German poet, a finicky modernist poet, a Cuban political poet, a handful of poets from around China, and me, the Black poet. Guan Guan was the elder poet.

My first day in Shanghai we were transported, gathered, and displayed "on behalf of all poets" at the World Poetry Forum Exhibition's "China and the Outside World: Reflections and Foresight upon a Century of Poetry." Guan Guan was already speaking or singing to all who listened, while the rest of us looked around in confusion. By *us* I mean me and everyone else in the crowded, anxious ballroom of Shanghai Jiao Tong University: a squad of jet-lagged international poets, some scribbling critics and scholars, a mix of staff and faculty and students, a few journalists, and camera crews tangled in wires. The people of China and the outside world spoke languages that were foreign to me, despite being translated here and there by my somber translator, who was something like a closet poet.

5

We were gathered to reflect on a century of poetry. When I got an email invitation to the festival from someone with a yahoo.com address, I thought it was some strange poetry scam.

Dear Sir/Madam:

Year of 1917 is marked as a new starting point for modern Chinese poetry, when vernacular poems by Hushi were published in the "New Youth"; in the same year, Thomas Stearns Eliot published his poem collection "Prufrock and Other Observations" which was regarded as a milestone in Western poetry history and inaugurated a new era for Western poetry. To honor the significance of these historical events, the 'World Poetry Forum' will be hosted during "The First Shanghai International Poetry Festival." In the perspective of world poetry, the Forum is intended to celebrate the hundred years' history of modern Chinese poetry as the representative achievement for the fascinating coincidence in Chinese and Western civilization history as well as Chinese and Western civilization exchange and learning. The Forum will also facilitate comprehensive and systematic studies and reflection on the hundred years' history of Chinese and Western poetry, summarize their historical development, primary achievements and current issues, and then look into their future development. We would like to invite you to the Forum, and your presence will be greatly appreciated.

The old English poet had a spouse in tow. The younger poets looked to party. The modernist poet complained about the hotel, the food, the weather. I hung between the famous Pulitzer poet and the lonely translator who whispered sidebars of gossip and judgment to me. I had been lonely long before Shanghai, so I wasn't lonely exactly. It was a pleasant sort of Babel in my view. I felt comfortably lost in translation. I never found out who was actually in charge of anything.

The festival attendees had been waiting impatiently for us. Many of the poets on our panel were well-known in China. We were all put on display immediately. We had ten minutes each to reflect on a century of poetry. The Cuban poet's reflections upon a century of poetry included a description of playwright and poet Federico García Lorca stroking the back of Salvador Dalí's long, veiny painting hand. He promised to settle once and for all the mysteries surrounding Lorca's death in 1936. He'd been betrayed by friends of the family. Franco ruled for thirty-nine years after Lorca was assassinated, the Cuban poet explained. The German poet read a few poems by Rainer Maria Rilke and then reflected on something Rilke said about Rodin: "He lived nothing that is not in his work." I told the poet translator that Gertrude Stein said, "It is always a mistake to be plainspoken." Eliot believed the same thing, though he'd have never admitted it.

I did just as the invitation letter said: I reflected very specifically on a century of American poetry. I said American poetry was born essentially of two streams: Emily Dickinson, the shy, private weirdo, and Walt Whitman, the public, social weirdo. I included some quotes reflective of their differing philosophies: "I dwell in possibility" versus "I contain multitudes." Next, Robert Frost was extending Whitman's appeal to the public body. There was no time to read "Stopping by Woods on a Snowy Evening." Around the same time T. S. Eliot came, despairing the diminishment of Waspy enlightenment. Modernism began, just as the letter suggested, in 1917 with Eliot, but also with World War I and the Great Migration of Black people from the South to the North.

Several Chinese college students sat along the walls. Older audience members sat in chairs encircling us. Many of the audience members wore earpieces. We were outfitted with microphones and headsets that translated our comments to Mandarin. Everyone remained in a cloud of confusion, as far as I could tell.

I said T. S. Eliot, straddling America and England, was a melancholy bridge between the old and modern worlds. The hundred years since 1917 included whatever we call the span between the modern and present. Not postmodern. Eliot marked the birth of modernism. He enlarged the fires stoked by Dickinson and Whitman. He was a banker, y'all. He made jobs for lots of poets. And lots of critics. And lots of colleges and businesses. He made a business of academic information. His actual poems articulate the modernist angst and anxiety of his existence; poetry as an escape from the no-longer-natural world to the world of the mind. I'm sure no one followed any of this. I imagine they wanted something particular to a Black poet and Black poetry. Given ten minutes, where would you begin your story of American poetry?

I never had a favorite Phillis Wheatley or Anne Bradstreet poem. It was the language of Keats and the rhythm of Whitman, the weird obstinacy of Dickinson, that interested the young poet in me. The old English poet nodded; the experimental poet frowned. No Eliot. The old English poet and modernist poet frowned. The modernist poet interrupted, "Stevens was not a modernist." Though nearly all of them exposed their racism privately. The famous Pulitzer poet nodded. Even Whitman, it turns out. Frowns all around. I only covered half a century of American poetry with my time. I didn't leave room for reading my poems. I had not started writing the American Sonnets. Donald Trump was a few months from being elected. I grew obsessed with creating my own condensed historical timeline of American poetry after that panel. In fact, the first poem of *American Sonnets for My Past and Future Assassin* alludes to my notion of lineage and ultimately, the influence of myth and memory over fact and history.

AMERICAN SONNET FOR MY PAST AND FUTURE ASSASSIN

> The black poet would love to say his century began
> With Hughes or God forbid, Wheatley, but actually
> It began with all the poetry weirdos & worriers, warriors,
> Poetry whiners & winos falling from ship bows, sunset
> Bridges & windows. In a second I'll tell you how little
> Writing rescues. My hunch is that Sylvia Plath was not
> Especially fun company. A drama queen, thin-skinned,
> And skittery, she thought her poems were ordinary.
> What do you call a visionary who does not recognize
> Her vision? Orpheus was alone when he invented writing.
> His manic drawing became a kind of writing when he sent
> His beloved a sketch of an eye with an X struck through it.
> He meant *I am blind without you*. She thought he meant
> *I never want to see you again*. It is possible he meant that, too.

Nearly all we invited poets had presented, and as far as I could tell, the audience remained in a collective confusion until Guan Guan spoke. His mouth made the sound of a bullfrog, then a lute or flute; then he was a strange, croaking wind instrument burping and cooing vowel and owl syllables. After two or three minutes of weird, wonderful, spiritual, sexual, playful, mournful performance, Guan Guan said, "I am a dog from heaven and I want to swallow the sun"—or that's what was translated to me by the translator while I also listened to someone else translate Guan Guan from Taiwanese to English in an earpiece.

My translator also listened through an earpiece as another translator said Guan Guan said, "The man who invented language gained God's favor."

"Probably this is incorrect," my translator whispered.

"God showered the man with fruit," the other translator said Guan Guan said.

"Language probably was not invented this way," my translator said.

"What way?" I whispered back. "How did he say it was invented?"

"Though the fruit, when it fell from the tree, fell in enough plentitude to feed everybody, but there was still envy," my translator translated with a simultaneous headshake.

"Language was invented by people, not one man," my translator said.

I asked again if Guan Guan said how exactly the man invented language. Was he a farmer or something? A magician? Hunter?

"Language was invented by people who'd learned to communicate using braids and knots of rope, not a *poet*," my translator said, in a half-sidebar mode.

A poet?

"One knot in a length of string was a yes, two a no, villages used them to communicate," my translator continued.

A poet? How? I asked.

"Guan Guan says the story proves a poet need not be someone who writes poetry," my translator said. Confusion clouded my brow.

Guan Guan's singing and chanting quieted after a succinct, hypnotizing ten minutes. Then he settled in his seat beside me and said in decent, creaky English, "The poet does not write poetry." He spoke

English but preferred the poetry of his own language and action, probably. He had starred in Asian movies as a young man at the turn of the century. I could not tell if he heard the translator muttering disagreement. His smile was warm and sly.

I saw Guan Guan buy peaches from a street vendor before we entered the Hot Pot to dine after the event. In the Hot Pot pots of boiling water sat on a hot plate at the center of the table, full of strips of beef. The poet translator translated the multi-language but mostly Mandarin conversation about the looming election of Donald Trump versus Hillary Clinton. Someone said Trump was good for America, he'd shake things up, probably. Maybe that was the translation. "When the wife of a president becomes the president, we call that a dynasty," the experimental poet said. "We call that fascism," the modernist said. "She's boring," the translator said or translated. Half the time I couldn't understand a single bit of what anybody was saying. More than half the time.

The modernist poet asked if we could be taken elsewhere to dine. No. First the modernist poet had gone on for too long talking about modernism, and now kept asking everyone to take selfies and swap emails. No, before that the modernist poet asked me to co-read a poem when we were on the panel. I said maybe, and when the poet turned I turned to the poet translator and said I didn't want to do such a thing. A large portion of life concerns the struggle between you and what other people want to do with your body. The modernist poet was the first among our party to leave the Hot Pot, but not before approaching each of us looking for another poetry gig. Might my school pay for a lecture in two departments, the English Department and Department of History? I said I didn't think so.

At the party Guan Guan smoked cigarettes, drank with the women, and shared his peaches. His face pinched and puckered around each cigarette like was sucking music out of it. The Beijing poet, who was also, possibly, a Guan Guan scholar, said the last time the elder poet was in Shanghai he boarded a ship to England. It was 1933, the year Eliot divorced his first wife. The young elder poet happened upon Eliot near a brothel. He asked Eliot if he might become his teacher. Eliot observed the young elder poet's getup. The Beijing poet said the elder poet wore the same old madcap outfits back then. Everyone laughed. The Beijing poet said something in Mandarin and everyone laughed again. Every poet but the elder poet mentioned T. S. Eliot, though the elder poet was the only one in the room to have met him.

On the first day of the Shanghai International Poetry Festival, the Beijing poet had gone well over time despite his charm. The German poet went well under. But the modernist poet went longest, talking twenty minutes and ending with an Eliot sentence from "The Love Song of J. Alfred Prufrock." It was a dazzling sentence: "The yellow fog that rubs its back upon the window-panes, / The yellow smoke that rubs its muzzle on the window-panes, / Licked its tongue into the corners of the evening, / Lingered upon the pools that stand in drains, / Let fall upon its back the soot that falls from chimneys, / Slipped by the terrace, made a sudden leap, / And seeing that it was a soft October night, / Curled once about the house, and fell asleep." Before departing and after relenting and trying the hot pot broth, the modernist poet lifted a ladle and a cuff rolled back to reveal a grave scar. The skin rose like a slug along the line between the palm and wrist. What does it mean to kiss the wounds of a failed suicide?

At the last event of the Shanghai International Poetry Festival, Guan Guan belted out a song once again, his old face wrinkled in effort. I was so inspired by him, I decided to sing my poem "Wind in a Box" to the audience. I wasn't sure anything else would translate. But I knew how I felt listening to Guan Guan sing at every opportunity. I wasn't sure how else to communicate I was a poet to the master elder. Afterward the poet translator asked if the poem was an elegy. No, I told her. I had written it before my marriage ended. The wind is the breath, the body is the box. I was just a Black man singing his heart out. Guan Guan gave me the courage to do it.

In one of China's ancient dynasties there was a building full of scientists, alchemists, wise men, and magicians researching the future. The power to control time is the sum of God's power over man, probably. All of the wisest, smartest men on the planet had been imprisoned in a great tower, an office building with more floors than stars in heaven. Or they were imprisoned in caves in a great mountain. The emperor said only the man to conquer the future could go free. The men worked long hours over long years for the answer. The emperor wanted to foresee his oversights, his downfall, his future betrayers. When the enemy shot arrows through all the windows of his palace, should he take up arms or should he sit down to write his son a letter? A family writes the same story over many years without ever actually reaching the story's conclusion.

I forgot to tell you about the guy I saw in the hotel mirror. After the festival I took a room on the sixth floor of a hotel near what they call Shanghai Times Square. One night when I looked from my hotel room window into the room of an adjacent hotel, I saw a man in his hotel room standing with his nose to the mirror for what felt like ten or fifteen minutes. He was alone, in a dark suit. He wasn't screaming. I didn't dream it. It was the madness of loneliness.

I think I fell in love once or twice along each of the dozen or so blocks I walked from Shanghai Times Square to Xintiandi, to the Huai-hai Middle Road residential district, to the crowed labyrinths and enclaves of Tianzifang. It was my last day in Shanghai. I did not have my camera, but my pockets were stuffed with money. The largest bill is worth about fifteen dollars in Shanghai. It takes a lot of them. I found small things as I wandered the vendor stalls: a wooden Buddha with a large head, some whatnots and souvenirs. I probably would not be able to find my way back to the stall of a petite, beautiful merchant. It was a dark room, the walls were gray, expensive dresses and shawls hung on the racks. Two boys played in a corner.

When all else failed the emperor visited the oldest poet alive. "Is poetry not a place to house the past? Might the poet also know a window on what's to come?" the emperor asked the elder poet. Guan Guan told us that after the man who invented language gained God's favor, ghosts began to appear. I won't be sure of anything, even if I live to be eighty-eight. Four in five poets believe ghosts communicate telepathically. Therefore you may never prove their existence. "Man, you too old to be so joyful," I said to Guan Guan when I realized he understood me. The poet need not write poems if the poet becomes a poem. Is a made thing ever more interesting than the maker of things? Not to me.

The Nine Muses of a Poetry Enthusiast's View Of History or the Nine Multi-faced, Multifaceted Muses of American Poetic Production?

CALLIOPE OR PHILLIS WHEATLEY?

THE MUSE INSIDE OR JEAN TOOMER?

THE MODERN DANCER OR SYLVIA PLATH?

THE MIND OR HIROSHIMA?

SHEPHERD OR THE MUSE OF FALLING AND CATCHING UP?

THE MUSE OF SPHINX HOWLS OR THE MOTHERS OF EMMETT TILL?

THE SPACE CHALLENGER OR THE MUSE IN MIKE TYSON?

SIREN OR THE MUSE OF MUSIC AND MOVIES?

THE MUSE OF TOMORROW OR THE STARS OF EROS AND PSYCHE?

OTHER USES OF MUSES?

DECIPHERING WHAT MAKES A POEM MOVE?

DICTION

IMAGERY

FORM

FIGURATIVE LANGUAGE

SOUND

SENTENCE

DECIPHERING WHAT MAKES A POEM MOVING?

CONTEXT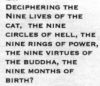

TEXT

SUBTEXT

OR DECIPHERING THE NINE LIVES OF THE CAT, THE NINE CIRCLES OF HELL, THE NINE RINGS OF POWER, THE NINE VIRTUES OF THE BUDDHA, THE NINE MONTHS OF BIRTH?

*Concerning the musing: Are the questions contained in this examination written to reflect the content or contentment of the poet? Can this examination provide an idea of general areas of strength and weakness in poetry? Can personal, cultural, and poetic questions impact the potential answers in life?

TWENTIETH CENTURY EXAMINATION

Part I: Where Would You Begin?

1900

Sigmund Freud's *Interpretation of Dreams*

1903

W. E. B. Du Bois publishes *The Souls of Black Folk*

1905

Albert Einstein's theory of relativity

1909

National Association for the Advancement of Colored People (NAACP) founded

1911

First Hollywood studio founded

1912

Poetry magazine founded

1913

The Armory Show: The International Exhibition of Modern Art

Robert Frost publishes *A Boy's Will* in London

1914–1918

World War I

1918

Influenza epidemic

Emily Dickinson
Musing on Possibility?

Walt Whitman
Musing on People?

Gertrude Stein ## Musing on Vocabulary?

Robert Frost
Musing on Frost?

1. If you decided to chart your genealogy according to the poets and poetry you know, would it be more comprehensive than what you know of your actual family?

2. If you were going to cover a hundred or so years of the history of something very important to you, would you begin with your muses?

3. Who in your poetic history is your muse of contradiction, or your muse of possibility, or your muse of eccentric verbal vocabulary?

4. What would John Keats think of jazz?

5. Who is the new modernist?

6. What would you find if you looked for yourself in poetry everyday?

7. Is a historian a caretaker?

8. Is what makes a hero heroic what makes a poet poetic?

9. What if Walt Whitman and Emily Dickinson dreamed the same dream one night in the summer of 1885?

10. Do you think history is a kind of extended public family rooted in the binaries of mother and father, yin and yang, moon and sun, song and story?

11. Are there other ways to synthesize a poetic genealogy?

12. Would you believe that in 1885 Whitman and Dickinson separately, simultaneously dreamed they were co-parents to a haunted Black orphan girl?

13. What happens if W. E. B. Du Bois's *The Souls of Black Folk* is considered the first hybrid poetry collection?

14. Can an entire people be the muse of colonization and industrialization, or the muse of fantasy and slavery?

15. Is it a help or hindrance to think of literary history as a kind of genealogy?

16. Can an entire nation have an entire people as their muse?

17. Can any truly diverse audience agree on anything?

18. Have you ever seen someone with a "Because I could not stop for Death" tattoo?

19. Is that a line about the motion of living?

20. Do you know what Dickinson means when she says, "'tis Centuries—and yet / Feels shorter than the Day"?

21. What makes any poem or poet the definitive poem or poet of an era?

22. "Won't you celebrate with me"—isn't that what Lucille Clifton says about not stopping for death?

23. Did you know that 1885 was the year Mark Twain published *The Adventures of Huckleberry Finn*?

24. Should Mark Twain, the quintessential canonical writer of American letters, have a cameo in the dream of Whitman, Dickinson, and a Black child resembling Phillis Wheatley?

25. Do you think Whitman is considered the father of the last hundred years of American poetry because he was innovative, or because he was a white man?

End of Twentieth Century Examination, Part I?

My Gwendolyn Brooks

for Toi Derricotte

The life and work of Gwendolyn Brooks covers more space and time than just about any other poet in modern American poetry: from gangbangers reading poems in her South Side living room to Susan Sontag waving her ass in Brooks's face during a writer's panel in Russia. "Ass-stounding," says Ms. Brooks, according to her second autobiography. Do you know this story? She's in Russia with Robert Bly, Susan Sontag, and some other important American writers when a Russian journalist asks her what it's like to be Black in America. Sontag proceeds to answer. Brooks interrupts for obvious reasons, and then an angered Sontag stands up and shakes her big white ass in the face of the calmly seated Gwendolyn Brooks(!). Gwendolyn Brooks, the neighborly, Pulitzer Prize–winning Black lady from the South Side of Chicago. Brooks doesn't reveal her answer to the question, only the audacity of Sontag. I can't tell whether Brooks is enraged, embarrassed, or flattered by Sontag's antics. Her prose, like her poetry, and I think even the warble of her voice, can feel astoundingly polytonal, shifting between shade and sincerity, craft and craftiness. How is it that she can be the most well-known poet with the most unread poems in modern American poetry? Her most anthologized and beloved poem, "We Real Cool," can turn four-year-olds into dynamic spoken-word artists. It can turn dynamic spoken-word artists into couplet-wielding scatting language poets. It can turn scatting language poets into little old Black ladies standing at the door of a pool hall called the Golden Shovel. I've written about the poem. I love its mutually formal, lyrical, social edge. It's as futuristic/radical as jazz when it's published in *The Bean Eaters* in 1960, a decade after she won the Pulitzer Prize for Poetry. Why don't more critics write about Brooks?

Where does Gwendolyn Brooks go in modern American poetry? Postwar American poetry? My own handmade timeline of American poetry starts with Dickinson and Whitman and ends with poets like me talking about poems in the university. She often goes unacknowledged the way caretakers and angels go unacknowledged. Brooks would be essential to the American literary canon even if all she did was publish *A Street in Bronzeville* in 1945. She would be essential to the American literary canon even if all she did was get Etheridge Knight writing poems in prison. Even if all she did was pay out of her own pocket to get Audre Lorde's second book published. Gwendolyn Brooks would be essential even if all she did was influence the ways we think about Blackness.

Toi, I'd given a considerable amount of thinking to the brilliant life of Gwendolyn Brooks before it occurred to me you have been my own personal Gwendolyn Brooks for the entirety of my life. You both are evidence that the secret to longevity is living a poetic life. I have had all the good fortune of a student who had never been without his best teacher. I'm to deliver a lecture on Brooks for the Poetry Society in the UK. If they want to know what's truly exceptional in American poetry, they should look at Gwendolyn Brooks and her literary sisters and daughters. Anyone looking for a view of American culture as Stuart Hall understood it ("experience lived, experience interpreted, experience defined") should study the perspectives of its most acute observers: Black women. They witness racism intensified by sexism, and sexism intensified by racism.

Brooks was a daughter of the Great Migration, moving from Topeka to Chicago as a baby, raised in the age of Prohibition when women got the right to vote; she was a child prodigy who began publishing poems at thirteen, who wrote fan letters to poets, who married a man who was an aspiring poet, who was a twenty-eight-year-old wife and mother living on the South Side of Chicago when *A Street in Bronzeville* debuted with Harper & Row in 1945. The book jacket copy begins, "In these poems of contemporary Negro life a new and talented young writer relates with sincerity, perception and stunning power her feelings about her people." Do you know the photo of young Brooks standing with Langston Hughes, *The Poetry of the Negro* floating between them like a baton? She is our direct line to Langston Hughes, who selected her work for a literary prize in 1940. He celebrated the publication of her debut in the *Chicago Defender* the final year of World War II: "This book is just about the biggest little two-dollar worth of intriguing reading found in bookshops these atomic days." Brooks threw Hughes a going-away party when he moved from Chicago.

Between the Harlem Renaissance and Motown was the Chicago Renaissance at the turn of the century. Brooks was a witness through every age. The title *A Street in Bronzeville* sort of said up front Gwendolyn Brooks was interested in her neighbors and corners. Growing up in Bronzeville, Brooks could have heard Louis Armstrong and His Stompers, featuring Earl "Fatha" Hines, and the teenage MC Cab Calloway at the Sunset Cafe. Nat King Cole, Jelly Roll Morton, and King Oliver carried music up and down Bronzeville. Her neighbors were some of the most miraculous Black people ever to walk the planet.

Had Brooks published no other book after *A Street in Bronzeville*, she would still be one of our great national treasures. The book remains simply mind-blowing in its formal and tonal range, its poetic dexterities, its slyness and grace. But it's even more mind-blowing for the attention the poems pay to the everyday. The poem "When You Have Forgotten Sunday: The Love Story" foregrounds it's everydayness in the title, for example. The poem's animated, dash-filled syntax unfolds like bedsheets and loose limbs. Pulitzer or not, her attention to interior spaces—to Black interior spaces—meant her work would be overlooked by her contemporaries at every age. *The New American Poetry, 1945–1960*, edited by Donald Allen in 1960, the same year Brooks published her third book, *The Bean Eaters*, covering the year of her debut, does not include Gwendolyn Brooks. Her absence makes anything Donald Allen observes about the era half-baked, half-cocked. Brooks also was not included in *Black Fire: An Anthology of Afro-American Writing*, edited by Amiri Baraka and Larry Neal in 1968. Baraka appears in Donald Allen's anthology as LeRoi Jones, the only Black poet included. Audre Lorde is also absent from *Black Fire*. The omission of these women dramatically shrinks the scope of what those brothers called Black Art. But it doesn't matter whether Allen or Baraka or other stripes of Canonical Gatekeepers acknowledge Brooks: she's got her eye on the future.

Perhaps both *The New American Poetry* and *Black Fire* considered Brooks, already fifty in 1967, a member of the literary establishment. She was not. She remained deeply tied to youth through her community poetry initiatives. "We Real Cool" is among the first poems to empathize with the young people who would power the Black Power Movement that powered parts of the Civil Rights Movement. One may assume the pool players at the Golden Shovel are Black in "We Real Cool," when one knows Brooks's South Side. She watches them from the door of the pool hall. They will "die soon" in wars, in prisons, in the neighborhoods undermined by government housing projects, in the hands of racists. Brooks's social concerns for Black people intensified just as the social endangerment intensified in the sixties. Within a few months in 1963 Medgar Evers was murdered in Mississippi and four girls, Cynthia Wesley, Carole Robertson, Addie Mae Collins, and Denise McNair, were murdered in Alabama. When Malcolm X was assassinated in 1965 the poet LeRoi Jones moved from Greenwich Village to Harlem, changed his name to Amiri Baraka, and became one of the founders of the Black Arts Movement. The movement put language to the anger of the era.

Discussing the movement at the historic 1994 Furious Flower Poetry Conference (named after lines in Brooks's "Second Sermon on the Warpland"), Baraka emphasized its aim to create Black art and Black institutions. In Chicago, Hoyt Fuller's *Negro Digest* published the poems and prose of voices in the movement. In Detroit, Dudley Randall founded Broadside Press. Brooks was a central figure in each instance, sending the work of young poets to the *Negro Digest* and Broadside Press and speaking, teaching, guiding. She encountered a dynamic thirty-four-year-old Amiri Baraka and his peers/followers when she attended Fisk University's Black Writers' Conference in 1967. "They wanted to write and to change things with the passion of their writing," she wrote in her 1972 autobiography, *Report from Part One*. The poems of *In the Mecca* capture the energies of 1968, its publication year. Her poetics take shape in what she calls the "kindergarten of new consciousness." It is not so much a transformation as an evolution, an intensification of attentions, that emerges in Brooks after the Fisk conference. *In the Mecca* looks directly at the new Blackness of the era. Brooks evolves from social to political urgency just as Jones/Baraka does. Her evolution mirrors the arc of the century. "Second Sermon on the Warpland," one of her extraordinary poems from the collection, is a kind of directive and manifesto for the new poets.

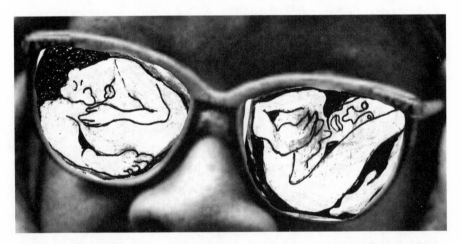

Brooks makes any conversation about American poetry of the last century more interesting. Brooks was born in 1917, the same year as Robert Lowell, who won the Pulitzer in 1947, three years before

Brooks. When he passed in 1977 Lowell was considered one of the chief poets of the twentieth century. He taught both Anne Sexton and Sylvia Plath. His family history could be traced back to the *Mayflower*.

As Robert Lowell is to Anne Sexton and Sylvia Plath, Brooks is to several generations of poets. Brooks met with James Baldwin and many Black poets of the era in her living room. I wish there was a better record of her relationship with Sonia Sanchez, their chats about motherhood, poetry, Blackness, community. Sonia Sanchez published her debut, *Homecoming*, in 1969, the same year Lucille Clifton published her debut, *Good Times*. Audre Lorde published *The First Cities*, her debut, in 1968. Brooks was a central figure in the work of all three poets.

Brooks meditates on what it means to be polytonally Black. Her definition evolves into something like a Pan-African Blackness in the 1980s when *The Near-Johannesburg Boy and Other Poems* is published. In a 1987 *Los Angeles Times* article, Brooks says hearing a radio broadcast of two Black South African boys asking each other, "Have you been detained yet? How many times have you been detained?" prompted her to write the title poem through the voice of a Black boy growing up outside the all-white town. The poem's slippery, sly mood is accentuated in Brooks's dynamic delivery. Her voice is enlarged when one hears recordings of her reading poems. When Brooks reads "We Real Cool," for example, she enlarges the "we" not only in her tone, but in her pitch and frequency. There is no recording of Brooks's strange exchange with Susan Sontag, but if you have ever heard Brooks speak you cannot unhear the switchblade of Black Woman wit in her speech In my recording of Brooks reading "The Near-Johannesburg Boy," her voice rings with overlapping shades and tones. Brooks's poems are forward-thinking in construction/conception while grounded in subject. She slides between registers of affection and caution and witness.

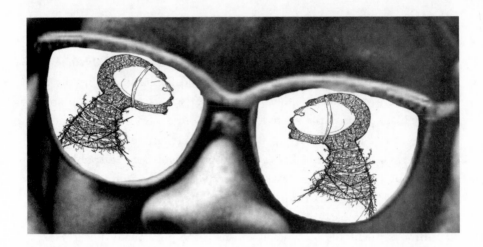

Legions of poets have been influenced by Brooks. I think of you and Rita Dove and Wanda Coleman as the daughters of Gwendolyn Brooks, a trio of sisters expressing their own frequencies of Blackness. I almost overlook Elizabeth Alexander, my spirit sister. Alexander has become a manifestation of Brooks's dream for us. A world where a poet—a Black woman poet—becomes a boss; a sister who runs shit. I almost forget to mention Elizabeth who is my Brooks shadow. Brooks wrote of marriage and motherhood before a word like *feminism* was in common usage. She wrote about the disappointments, dreams, and desires of gender and race with tenderness and scrutiny.

Do you think Gwendolyn Brooks would have received the Nobel Prize in Literature had an appropriate account been given? Isn't she our Wisława Szymborska, our Pablo Neruda? Around Chicago, community centers, schools, and publishing houses have been raised up to honor Brooks. Adults who dreamed of becoming poets as children report of letters sent to them and checks signed by Brooks. Patricia Smith may possess a stack of letters and certificates signed by Gwendolyn Brooks. Smith, one of the greatest contemporary poets in America, has to be among the truest and clearest of Brooks's descendants. The great Patricia Smith extends the reach of Brooks. In "After the Gwendolyn Brooks Reading," you depict Brooks bowed under wings of compassion, listening to chirping Black church ladies at a book signing table. Her influence rings in your poetry and affection. Near the end of "Black-bottom," you reconfigure the anaphoric we of Brooks's "We Real Cool" into the voices lost in the purgatorial suburbs: "We rolled our windows down . . . We hoped to pass invisibly, knowing . . . we would return safely . . . We wanted our sufferings . . . We had lost our voice . . . we had lost the right to sing . . ." You are one of Brooks's chief daughters. You both are evidence a Blackness rooted in intimacy must also be rooted in community. You have shown me one who lives as a poet is one who bears witness. Anyone looking for what's truly exceptional in American poetry should look at the Black women poets.

William Waring Cuney,
Born 1906

William Waring Cuney may have been nicknamed "Willy the War-
bler" before his retreat to quiet. He was educated at Lincoln University; the name of the man assassinated for speaking on Blacks' behalf
notarizes Cuney's degree. He decided to pursue singing in the New
England Conservatory of Music in Boston & from there went to Rome,
but Cuney never performed professionally. His claim to fame should
be he never sang for money before his retreat. His claim to fame should
be he wrote "No Images" at eighteen. During World War II, Cuney
served in the South Pacific as a technical sergeant. His claim to fame
should be he earned three Bronze Stars. His claim to fame should be

his "Southern Exposure" was set to music by Al Haig & Nina Simone. His claim to fame should be "Oh, my lord / what a morning, / Oh, my lord, what a feeling." Cuney offered words on the bricks of Blacks in the Bronx, the rings of Jack Johnson, Jesus, & the small talk curbing the crosswalks. *Puzzles* & stacks of *Storefront Church* sat in the bookstore that became a storefront church every night of the month. Cuney entered a self-sequestered quarantine from poets, friends, & the general public in the year John Glenn became the first American to orbit the earth. What Cuney felt upon the death of Langston Hughes, Malcolm X, MLK, & JFK, about the warring factions of sports teams & countries, songs & movies, et cetera, could have been his claim. When John Oliver Killens insulted Cuney's reputation in 1972, four years before his death, Cuney reemerged to respond ironically or irreverently or simply with ire. It should have been his claim to fame.

Margaret Danner,
Born 1915

The Langston Hughes Review was published literally & later conceptually by the indivisible, invisible members of the Langston Hughes Society, who appeared & disappeared reciting Hughes poems by heart in the record stores of Harlem every year on his birthday. Members seek the rare 1964 *Poets of the Revolution* record on Motown starring Langston Hughes & Margaret Danner: the Hughes superfan Black woman poet & member of the original unofficial Chicago South Side Community Poetry Workshop chapter of the Langston Hughes Society, with her slightly younger South Side neighbor & probable antagonist & friend Gwendolyn Brooks. Danner won second place at Northwestern's Poetry Workshop of the Midwestern Writers Conference in 1945, the same year Brooks published *A Street in Bronzeville*. When Margaret

Danner is on her way to record with Langston Hughes in 1964, she stops in the park to read her bundle of letters from Hughes, smelling possibly like his wrist. Danner includes all of her poems for Hughes in *The Down of a Thistle: Selected Poems, Prose Poems, and Songs*, published . in 1976, eight years before her death in 1984. Margaret Esse Danner, born in 1915 in Pryorsburg, Kentucky, to Caleb & Naomi Danner, but known to insist she was born in Chicago, holds the distinction of publishing more poems celebrating Langston Hughes than any other poet of the twentieth century.

POET ★ AA ALL STAR ★

MARI EVANS

Mari Evans,
Born 1919

From 1968 to 1973, during prime time on WTTV Channel 4, India-napolis, Mari Evans, poet, writer, activist, host with no background in television, transmitted *The Black Experience* to the 115,000 Negroes of Indianapolis as well as any other local & regional interested parties. Possibly, white farmers listened to Mari Evans to hear Wes Montgomery's guitar or Mari Evans herself humming at her piano. Possibly the camera cut from the piano keys to the old typewriter Evans made sing & cry at the Indiana Housing Authority. We do not know if Mari Evans held hands with the man or woman holding the handheld camera, shifting between long shots & wide angles of *The Black Experience*. Mari Evans published *Where Is All the Music?* in 1968 & the celebrated *I Am a Black Woman* in 1970. Let there be close-ups of *The Black*

Experience basking viewers who have never seen Black people in the transmissions of light & sound both produced by & emanating from Mari Evans. Evans also published *Singing Black: Alternative Nursery Rhymes for Children* in 1976 & *Black Women Writers (1950–1980): A Critical Evaluation* in 1984. Let *The Black Experience* be seen as a cloud of smoke from the mills. Let the camera cut to a cloud coughing from the stove or chimney of Blacks in a modest house. Then to a cloud above the mouths of Black men on a porch. Let the camera cut from the conversation to sunlight piercing the clouds, before cutting to Mari Evans, at age ninety-seven, smiling sternly at the camera & wishing Black people a good night.

Wallace Stevens Key

STEVENS SNOW CENTO

One must have a mind of winter
To regard the frost and boughs
Of the pine-trees crusted with snow
The light in the room more like a snowy air
Reflecting snow
And roses frail as April snow
Passions of rain or moods in falling snow
The sea is in the falling snow
On the surface of the water
And in the edges of the snow
This robe of snow and winter stars
Fetched up with snow that never falls to earth
Like the last muting of winter as it ends
At the earliest ending of winter
The wise man avenges by building his city in snow
As the mind to find what will suffice destroys
Romantic tenements of rose and ice
It was snowing
And it was going to snow
It will burst into flames
Either now or tomorrow or the day after that

*Cento of lines from *The Collected Poems of Wallace Stevens* (Vintage Books): Lines 1–3: "The Snow Man," Lines 4–5: "The Poems of our Climate," Line 6: "Cy est Pourtraicte, Madame Ste Ursule, et les Unze Mille Vierges," Line 7: "Sunday Morning," Line 8: "The Man with the Blue Guitar," Lines 9–10: "Tattoo," Line 11: "Snow and Stars," Line 12: "The Dove In The Belly," Line 13: "Looking Across The Fields And Watching The Birds Fly," Line 14: "Not Ideas About The Thing But The Thing Itself," Line 15: "Like Decorations In A Nigger Cemetery, " Lines 16–17: "Man and Bottle," Lines 18–19: "Thirteen Ways of Looking at A Blackbird," Lines 20–21: "Girl In A Nightgown."

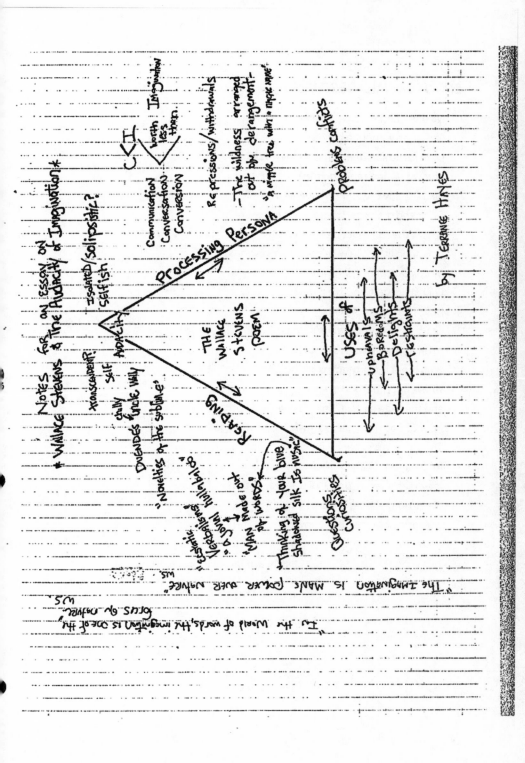

* Wallace Stevens Notes for an Essay on * The Audacity of Imagination *

CCH
North less Inspiration than.

Communication
Conversation
Conversion

Repressions/withdrawals

— The wildness arranged out by derangement.
"A mighty tree with a mighty nerve"

Processing Persona

isolated/solipsistic? selfish

Approach

transcendent self

chilly Uncle Wally

DUENDES

"Novelties of the sublime"

Verbalisms of a Sequel of hilarious
eestatic
"MAN made out of words"

Thinking of your blue Shadowed silk is music

Reading

THE WALLACE STEVENS POEM

Questions Curiosities

Problems conflicts

Uses of
Upheavals
Boredoms
Delights
Restraints

by Terrance Hayes

"The IMAGINATION IS MANS POWER OVER NATURE" — ws

"In the world of words, the imagination is one of the forces of nature." — ws

SNOW FOR WALLACE STEVENS

No one living a snowed in life
can sleep without a blindfold.
Light is the lion that comes down to drink.
I know *tink and tank and tunk-a-tunk-tunk*
holds nearly the same sound as a bottle.
Drink and drank and drunk-a-drunk-drunk,
light is the lion that comes down.
This song is for *the wise man who avenges*
by building his city in snow.
For his decorations in a nigger cemetery.
How, with pipes of winter
lining his cognition, does someone learn
to bring a sentence to its knees?
Who is not more than his limitations,
who is not the blood in a wine barrel
and the wine as well? I too, having lost faith
in language have placed my faith in language.
Thus, I have a capacity for love without
forgiveness. This song is for my foe,
the clean shaven, gray-suited, gray patron
of Hartford, the emperor of whiteness
blue as a body made of snow.

Reprinted from *Lighthead* (2010, Penguin)

TWENTIETH CENTURY EXAMINATION

Part II: Did Modernism Begin at the Same Time as American Poetry, or Vice Versa?

1920

Women's right to vote

1922

T. S. Eliot publishes *The Waste Land*

Claude McKay publishes *Harlem Shadows*

James Weldon Johnson publishes *The Book of American Negro Poetry*

Gertrude Stein publishes *Geography and Plays*

The first Pulitzer Prize for Poetry goes to Edwin Arlington Robinson

1923

William Carlos Williams publishes *Spring and All*

Wallace Stevens publishes *Harmonium*

Jean Toomer publishes *Cane*

1924

Marianne Moore publishes *Observations*

1926

Langston Hughes publishes *The Weary Blues*

1927

First talking movie: *The Jazz Singer*

1929

Stock market crash

Wallace Stevens
Musing on Snow?

William Carlos Williams
Musing on Things?

A young **Langston Hughes** Musing on *The Weary Blues*?

26. Would you rather be the first or the best at something?

27. Is Sigmund Freud's *The Interpretation of Dreams* a metaphor for poetry, or is poetry a metaphor for Sigmund Freud's interpretation of dreams?

28. Who, if not Emily Dickinson, is mother of the modern and contemporary American lyric poem, a poem that can sound like a letter from and to the self, a measure of consciousness?

29. Would you say Jorie Graham, Louise Glück, the late, great C. D. Wright, and late, great Lucie Brock-Broido are evidence of Emily Dickinson's influence on a generation of contemporary women poets, or would you say *white* women poets?

30. Is there no real sense of Dickinson's influence until after the poems her editor, Thomas Wentworth Higginson, manhandled and published after her death were replaced with a complete and reportedly less manhandled version sixty-five years later, in 1955?

31. What if that had happened earlier?

32. Is Einstein's theory of relativity a metaphor for poetry, or is poetry a metaphor for Einstein's theory of relativity?

33. Is it Walt, the wild-haired American Orpheus roaming battlefields in a beard of daffodils, and Emily, the demure American Eurydice by the window with her books, who raise this Black girl whose parents were kidnapped, enslaved, and disappeared?

34. What are your adjectives?

35. Is it Walt, the seabound Ulysses shrouded in sails, costarring with Emily, the housebound Penelope shrouded in shawls?

36. Is it better to write or receive a poem on your birthday?

37. Who was reading Emily Dickinson before World War II?

38. She's not mentioned in the letters or poems of Gertrude Stein or Edna St. Vincent Millay or Marianne Moore, is she?

39. Couldn't we update our poetry TV series with new generations of poets each season?

40. How about setting season two in England with Gertrude Stein and her brother, Robert Frost's entire family, Ezra Pound, and H.D.?

41. Couldn't we feature the 1913 Armory Show and have Harriet Tubman meet Picasso there?

42. Isn't the language you use rooted in a specific history?

43. Who is the better muse to *The Waste Land*: T. S. Eliot, or the Eliot fan who knows *The Waste Land* by heart?

44. Are you able to recite any poems by heart?

45. Should all the elementary schools make third graders memorize Robert Frost's 1923 poem "Stopping by Woods on a Snowy Evening"?

46. Should we all carry in our hearts the line, "Whose woods these are I think I know"?

47. Is a caretaker an archivist?

48. Do you feel you dwell in possibility too?

49. Who knows what William Carlos Williams thought of Ezra Pound's conspiring to outwit and out-waltz Walt Whitman in 1902?

50. Did you know Ezra Pound met Emmett Till's father in prison?

End of Twentieth Century Examination, Part II?

Poetry Foundation Journal Days, 2006

Journal Day One, June 5, 2006

A fear of boredom (what's the medical term for that?) compels me to try something different every day here: lists; imaginary poems, novels, and essays; little book reviews. We'll see. I'm currently teaching a poetry seminar in Lewisburg, Pennsylvania, and maybe that alone will be enough to blog about. For example, I gave a lecture on the tension between voice and craft a day ago. (Let me know if this bores you.) (I love parentheses.) Ever since an epic discussion-disguised-as-debate I had with my friend Renegade, I've been thinking about it. He believes there are specific principles to what constitutes a great poem (or work of art). I disagree. "There are many forms of great, many ways to be great," I told him. "Claiming there's a set of predetermined principles—that's too conservative for my tastes," I said. (Note: You should never call someone named Renegade "conservative." Nor should you imply another poet is not thinking like an artist. He's kind of stopped speaking to me because of it.)

Yesterday I was listening to a podcast (like blogs, they are a form of tedium that can occasionally be enriching) on *Science and the City* where V. S. Ramachandran gave a lecture on "Synesthesia and the Universal Principles of Art." He claimed in the more speculative part of his talk that principles like peak shifting, grouping, and isolation determine how we judge and respond to art. All very compelling, but for me, Renegade and this dude are talking about art from the outside, from the perspective of the gazer/audience, not the artist. Even if it's misguided, the artist needs a healthy sense of individuality to sustain his or her imagination. The "principles of art" might help guide the imagination, but they should not determine it. Shouldn't we say as much about *craft*, the most-used word (other than *poem*) in poetry workshops everywhere? Craft is a guide, not a formula. The elements of craft are how we know we're reading a poem and not a short story or newspaper article. Even in prose poems, examining the elements of craft (tone especially, but also imagery, metaphor, and structure, if not form) tells us whether we're looking at a poem or a prose paragraph. Discussing craft allows us to break poems into parts: the frequencies of diction and meter, the concrete blocks of imagery, the equations of metaphor. Craft gets at the science and engineering of poetry. It makes poems machines. And though I'm about to tell you poems are not mere machines, I fully acknowledge the value of talking about them this way. Craft gives us a common language, common tools. It also gives the teacher a way to measure and evaluate poems. Evaluation is easier when one sees poems as machines. But if a poem is a machine, it's an animal too—depending on your stance, an animal with a machine skeleton (say Steve Austin, the bionic man) or a machine shell with an animal heart (say Robocop). I'll say here that I think the poem is mostly an animal. We work to tame it, to train it, but ultimately it has a mind of its own. It's a child we're raising, a child we birthed and are responsible for, but a child we do not "own." And if it's alive (language is alive, right?), we can't just saw off a leg without ramifications. In fact, if it's an animal, we accept it even if one leg is shorter than the other. (One of Jesse Owens's legs was shorter than the other, and look how far and fast it got him.) If the poem is an animal, we are not after per-fection (the thing we are after if we view it as a machine); we are after what a parent is after. We are helping the poem discover its dream. Every poem has a dream. Hell, every word has a dream that, as far as I can tell, might best be described as a wish to be useful, indispensable, maybe unique. Renegade wasn't hearing this. Once he and I argued late into the night (argued until I lost my voice) about whether or not

Billie Holiday was a great singer. He said, in what I remember now as the voice of Mr. Spock, that she might have been a great stylist, but that her singing was never technically correct. Her poor technique had, in fact, ruined her voice, he said. I don't think Billie Holiday was after "craft" or technique. Maybe this is too romantic, but I think she was after something beyond craft. And I'm suggesting that there is something beyond craft where poetry is concerned too. Has to be. Otherwise a mastery of craft would mean a mastery of the poem. We'd expect a mature poet with control over "the principles of craft" to never write poorly. With the exception of Stanley Kunitz, most poets seem to get worse as they "mature," not better.

In the lecture I brought in poems by poets who demonstrated a "mastery" of craft in their first books, but inevitably moved beyond craft to something else. Amiri Baraka is an easy example. The poems in 1961's *Preface to a Twenty Volume Suicide Note* show that he obviously knows (or knew) "the rules." The first five lines of the title poem:

Lately, I've become accustomed to the way
The ground opens up and envelops me
Each time I go out to walk the dog.
Or the broad-edged silly music the wind
Makes when I run for a bus . . .

But five years later with "Black Art" he announced that he was after something else. The first lines of the poem:

Poems are bullshit unless they are
teeth or trees or lemons piled
on a step. Or black ladies dying
of men leaving nickel hearts
beating them down. Fuck poems

Which is better depends on your tastes, I suppose. I tried to tell Renegade I was less interested in good/great versus bad than in the relationship between craft and voice; tangible and intangible. One of the reasons we don't talk much about voice is its slippery, atmospheric quality. It's a close cousin to tone, which is maybe the most difficult of the craft elements to teach. Tone and voice are matters of sensibility. You can't teach sensibility, can you? Maybe sensibility can only be shaped/filtered through craft: sometimes enlarged by it, sometimes obscured. (I love the word *maybe* only slightly more than I love the word *perhaps*.) Tell me how you'd define voice in poetry? Tell me in a way that would make it useful to students. Tell me in a way that would convince Renegade. Maybe we don't even have a good definition of craft yet. I'd vote for adding culture as an element, for example.

Where would you discuss the influences of race, class, and gender on theme and language if not in a discussion of craft? Including culture as an element helps me argue for the poems Baraka has been writing since "Black Art" as poems, not polemics with line breaks. His infamous poem "Somebody Blew Up America" makes use of all kinds of figures of speech—especially irony ("Who the richest / Who say you ugly and they the good lookingest")—even if ultimately those elements are funneled toward a particular (polemical) intention. Intention is, perhaps, closer to function than craft because it involves a poem's purpose; it involves how the writer intends the poem to "function" for readers. (Perhaps craft should/does help one discover function and intention.) "Somebody Blew Up America" lacks consistency, but it does not lack craft. It possesses a clear voice (Baraka persona), but the articulation (construction) of voice is not necessarily independent of craft. It's a matter of which comes first, maybe.

At what point does craft (the principles of poetry) give way to voice (the sensibilities of imagination)? And vice versa: When does/should the imagination (voice) give way to the principles (craft) that guide a reader through the poem? (Say, maybe it's called *craft* because it's what transports the language.) I'm thinking of folk like Wallace Stevens, Frank O'Hara, and Lucille Clifton. Aren't their best poems the ones that "match the rhythms of their strides"—to adapt a Wally Stevens line? Shouldn't we be wary of any "principles" that flatten or normalize those rhythms? Shrug. I could go on, but what would I have to talk about tomorrow? I'm gonna call Renegade soon. Sooner or later. . . .

Journal Day Two, June 6, 2006

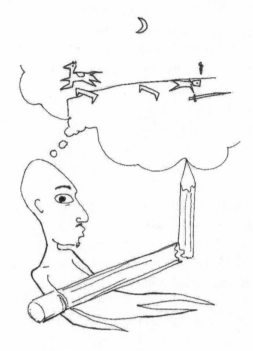

First off, sorry about that long-ass blog yesterday. Performance anxiety. I plan to write less and less each day. Maybe just my name by the end of the week.

I jerked upright in bed somewhere around six a.m. today and blurted, "Chuck Norris!" to an empty room in an empty house. Maybe I thought someone was lurking about. All day I've been troubling myself with why it was Chuck Norris (and not Bruce Lee or Jim Kelly). He's a Republican, I think. And with each year more and more strange looking. An image of Chuck Norris decapitating (dechoppitating?) a bad guy's head is among my earliest memories of drive-in movie nights with my parents. I assume my parents took me with them to see such things because they thought I'd forget them. They were partly right. I only remembered enough to constitute occasional nightmares, enough to constitute a worldview that is mostly dream. Do you, too, believe surrealism is often more real than realism? What was Plato thinking to distrust "reality" in the hands of artists?

I ask because I brought Anne Carson's *Economy of the Unlost: Reading Simonides of Keos with Paul Celan* (Princeton University Press, 1999) along with me to Lewisburg. It's a terrific book. A mix of classics, history lesson, and philosophy, which I realize describes lots of her work. She shows us how poems are the most polymorphous/polytypic of literary forms: they can be or blend the techniques of journalism, fiction, theater, cinema, manuals, on and on. (Where are the science-fiction poems: automatons, cone-shaped rockets, women with three eyes and men with none?) In a section called "APATE (the art of deception)," she says Plato "deplored poetry all the way back to Homer, [because] it cut words free from any obligation to reality." This may be a simplified translation of Plato (simplified by my hands, not Carson's, no doubt), but I'm drawn to questions of reality versus deception in art. Elsewhere in the chapter she says Gorgias, the sophist, believed the word that tricks you is more just than the word that does not. "Teachers like Gorgias and Protagoras alleged that the proper activity of words is not to describe but to deceive."

I said as an aside yesterday that there is a relationship between craft and function. A few questions: Does the political poet place function beside craft, if not before it? Is poetry that directly engages in political discourse deceptive? Are poems about personal subjects (family, gardens, sunsets) "benevolent" deceptions? Baldwin said something like art is that which reveals the questions hidden by the answers, so I figured I'd just ask, not attempt to answer. (Can a question deceive?) I want to believe it's only "deception" when the artist lacks morality. Is all true/great/enduring art moral art? You ask, "What do you mean by 'morality'?" and I ask, "What does Plato mean by 'reality'?" Is reality (which is not the same thing as science) more subjective than morality (which is not the same thing as religion)? These are questions worth wrestling with—maybe just outside the door of poetry.

Really, reading Anne Carson (and the writer Rebecca Solnit; check out *Wanderlust* and *A Field Guide to Getting Lost*), I am overcome with the wish to weave such questions into the fabric of a poem. Poems can hold anything. I also want to poke Plato in the eye and cut the imagination free of any obligations to reality. Hell, reality makes me want to do it! And yet I know catchphrases like "Weapons of Mass Destruction," "War on Terror," "Commander in Chief," "Land of the Free" magnify the problems with cutting words free. Are politicians the poets Plato was thinking of? The word that tricks you is not always just, Gorgias. Language is deceptive, yes. It is only occasionally a deception.

Journal Day Three, June 7, 2006

What does the internet, with its boundless resources, mean to the poet compelled to turn information into imagery and ideas? Maybe this could describe all poets. Surely someone somewhere has discussed this question once or twice. Last fall when Yona entered a library science master's program (in part to get away from the goo attached to living as a poet and teacher of poetry), one of our first discussions/debates concerned what the internet means for the library. I argued that the library was on its way to becoming a kind of museum; that its role as a locus for information was being replaced by the internet. She disagreed, not only because of the class presumptions I was making (not everyone can afford computers and internet), but because I had no idea what was going on in today's libraries. I was/am mostly at the keyboard. True, true, but I'm on a tangent here. (Plus, I lost the debate.)

I find the kinds of information online both overwhelming and endlessly interesting. Today, when a student read a poem framed by a fairly obscure religious reference, another student admitted to using Wikipedia to learn about it. I and half the class chimed, "Ah, Wikipedia," while the other half stared blankly.

[Commercial break: Students invariably ask how important it is to know all of a poem's references and allusions. My response: One can admire/appreciate a portrait (for its brushstroke, composition, color, etc.) without knowing who the subject of the painting is. If the painting is no good, knowing who the subject is doesn't make it better; if it is good, knowing the subject enriches the experience.]

"You may not like my stuff; I'm kind of a nature poet," a student said at the beginning of our conference today. I instantly wondered which of my anti-nature poems she'd been reading. "A good poem is a good poem," I said, even as I wondered who decides the "kind" of poet we are to be? The poet Robert Wrigley lives in rural Idaho (all of Idaho is rural) and often writes about animals. His book titles, for example, include *Lives of the Animals* and *Reign of Snakes*. And the big clue: in his author photos he's often outside! Still, I knew I'd made a mistake calling him "a nature poet" to his face once. I backtracked: "Oh, yes, there's a lot of other stuff in your poems, my bad." Fitting Wrigley on the Nature shelf is as problematic as fitting me on the—actually, I don't know the name of my shelf. . . .

Can the poet claim a style and still claim to resist categorization? Should a poet bother claiming a style? (No.) If categories are unavoidable, does it make more sense to categorize the style of the poem and not the style of the poet? Writing nature poems does not make one a nature poet, just as a poet who experiments is not necessarily experimental. It makes sense that a poet would resist these labels, if only because they imply one's approach to poetry is fixed.

The wish to categorize may be an inherent part of reading and comprehension. Maybe it's bound to a wish for clarity—a clear sense of order (organization/direction). More often than not, categories lead to presumptions. The easiest example would be the problems in reading a lyric poem as if it were a narrative poem. Since a poem rarely announces itself as narrative or lyric, a reader can be forgiven for making certain assumptions before entering a poem. But to exit a poem with the same assumptions is obviously a fairly limited engagement.

What seems to be an effort to comprehend is often an effort to impose a narrow meaning or to strip meaning away. I'm thinking about the dynamics of the typical workshop, but I'm also thinking about the broader implications of a fixed "standard of excellence" in art. Such an illusion of good and bad allows a reader to insist the problems are always with the poem and not, at least to some degree, with how the reader has read the poem. It is like listening to classical music and saying it's bad because it's not rap or rock. Obviously, as a different style of music, it requires a different set of criteria.

The way we judge a "nature poem" should not be the way we judge what I've heard called an "urban poem." (Did you know *urban* replaced *inner city*, which replaced *ghetto*, which replaced *Black*?) I'd argue that even the criteria specific to a "performance poem" differ from the criteria specific to a "spoken-word poem." Of course, such an array of styles means a reader is expected to constantly shift and mix perspectives. Not just from style to style, but poem to poem. That's a good thing. Jay-Z has been mixed with the Beatles; Biggie Smalls has been mixed with Frank Sinatra—it is possible to value two very different things at once. No reader should want a poet to be one thing. No poet should want to be one thing, to have one style. This is why we're looking for the "urban nature poem" (I think Major Jackson's Urban Renewal poems come closest to such a thing). And we're looking for the child of Gertrude Stein and Billy Collins, the child of Lucille Clifton and Wallace Stevens. Imagine those children. Imagine their poems.

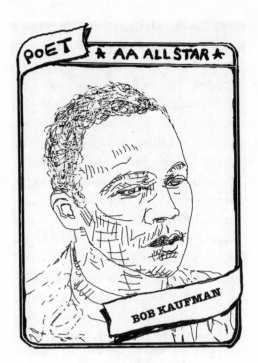

Bob Kaufman,
Born 1925

When Bob Kaufman dies, at age sixty in 1986, from a condition in which the liver does not live properly due to long-term trauma, the ghosts he meets traveling the road from San Francisco back to New Orleans call him "the Buddha Fly," because he is pajamaed in a burlap robe & holds a quill made of a crow feather in his writing hand & a writhing crow in the other. A transient cloud defecting to God while lambasting the Fifth Commandment like Noah shipwrecked & gnawing his nails with his wisdom teeth, Kaufman was thin as a skeleton transported to the realm of symbolic meaning. It was the middle of a triple-digit July. A gate swung between café excursions & nights of smothered rage, spontaneous revelations exploding into Birdland saxophone refrains, black rain falling on the snow, the ancient rain falling on the maternal from a distant American sky crackling with eclipses, commuted bluenesses, footpaths hidden beneath shadows, shivers impaled on slivers of wind in silver traffic, impaled on the nautical sounds of weeping & sweating. A pregnant tongue bounced up & down like a merchant marine counting vultures & stars from the deck of a sinking ship in the mouth of Bob Kaufman. He wouldn't put the quill & crow down even when the ghosts offered him shade & drinkable rain.

Russell Atkins,
Born 1926

The practice of a poem should be what archaeology makes you feel glowing red in a darkroom. Art should encourage expenditures of beasts buried with candelabras burning elaborately underground. Rhythm need not table panic. It's warm. Type *prototype* versus *stereotype* in a letter to Marianne Moore on her deathbed & await her reply. Every word was air when the zeitgeist was no more Mr. Nice Guy. If you get to Moscow on a song you will be soaked in a rain of applause unless there is snow. There must be stretches of your own colorful moonlight operatic combustions breaking gently from the speakers of postindustrial Cleveland. Do not allow surprise agony to quiet. Rhythm need not table panic. Art, you realize, does not explain taxonomy, Antarctica, lavender. Ghosts rest in the nest. A blood of lighter fluid makes you perspire. The fear inside the lonely cloud consumed by the lake. Vainly restrict sinking, garbling, or gulping garbage worth incalculable miscalculations. One transparent word rushed toward the unyielding ear. Is a window a shimmering shard of rain hung from a blue wall? Is a poem the practice of anything struck out & lifted with the fingertips? Russell Atkins awaits Marianne's reply.

POET ★ AA ALL STAR ★

RAYMOND PATTERSON

Raymond Patterson, Born 1929

Born in Harlem, Raymond Patterson is not considered a New York School poet despite living in New York most of his life. His poem "Twenty-Six Ways of Looking at a Blackman" suggests it takes twice the power of Stevens's imagination to make a Black man a Blackman. Where Stevens relies, per usual, on enough images of snow to cover twenty mountains, Patterson relies on the color that fills the fields, the concentric pebbles & the vagrancies of midnight. A Black man is spotted crossing the road holding a jackhammer, a grocery bag, the hand of his daughter, the jacket of his wife. Before settling on the number twenty-six Patterson considered a twenty-seventh Black man shocked by the scale of the auction block & a twenty-eighth shocked by the blade in the blood on the whip. Back & forth a twenty-second Black man goes, harvesting the vines growing toward the light & the roots growing toward the darkness. A thirty-first Black man carries bruised apples for his children. He takes an apple for himself, pressing slightly into an indentation, the meat gone brown beneath the skin. What grave, terrible thing happened to my boyhood friend between middle school & middle age to change him? When I met him twenty years later, he still had the same skin. His father used to drive a truck, his mother was a ghost, his little sister looked up to him. A shy chuckle used to echo like a rock over the water in him. When I met him we were kind to each other, older, but no longer kin. I could not fathom how he'd become the kind of Black man he was nor what he thought was Black in him.

TWENTIETH CENTURY EXAMINATION

Part III: Why So Few Poems Concerning the Atomic Bomb?

1930

Hart Crane publishes *The Bridge*

1935–1945

Works Progress Administration:
WPA & New Deal

1936

Iowa Writers' Workshop founded

1940

Richard Wright publishes *Native Son*

1941

US enters World War II following the
Japanese attack on Pearl Harbor

1942

Margaret Walker wins the Yale
Younger Poets Prize for "For My
People"

1945

Gwendolyn Brooks publishes
A Street In Bronzeville

The United States detonates atomic
bombs over Hiroshima and Nagasaki

1947

Anne Frank's *The Diary of a Young Girl*

1948

T. S. Eliot awarded the Nobel Prize
in Literature

1949

Arthur Miller publishes
Death of a Salesman

Langston Hughes
Musing on a Montage of Dreams Deferred?

The American Muse of Destruction
with the First Atomic Bomb?

Gwendolyn Brooks
Musing on Her Neighbors?

51. If you were going to cover one hundred or so years of your poetic history, would your timeline include Paul Laurence Dunbar, two years younger than and just as dark as Robert Frost?

52. Is the poetic canon essentially a poet's Hall of Fame, where members are voted in by peers and scholars?

53. If William Carlos Williams was a doctor, Wallace Stevens was a vice president at an insurance company, Frost was a landowner, Eliot was a banker, and Stein had enough money to live in Paris, how many poets in the canon were actually poor?

54. Which canonical poets wrote best about class?

55. Which canonical poets wrote best about sex?

56. What happens when a young, nomadic Langston Hughes is the star of season two, and he crosses paths with Allen Ginsberg in Williams Carlos Williams's doctor's office in 1930, when Ginsberg is four?

57. Is it a help or hindrance to think of literary history as a series of biographical episodes?

58. Where are the World War I and World War II poems by William Carlos Williams and Wallace Stevens?

59. There will be fun to be had with the end of Prohibition, but wouldn't war and the Great Depression be a big part of a situation comedy about poetry in the 1920s?

60. In her 1924 collection, *Observations*, does Marianne Moore have any observations about going to vote after the women's suffrage law was passed in 1920?

61. Are we sold on Marianne Moore's authenticity of spirit because she articulates her spirit so well in her poems?

62. Did you know the US Constitution makes no mention of the right to privacy?

63. Who can forget a name like John Crowe Ransom?

64. Doesn't World War I almost overshadow the 1918 influenza pandemic the way COVID-19 almost overshadowed our world's wars?

65. What do you know about Gertrude Stein's influence on Picasso?

66. What do you think William Carlos Williams means when he says, "What

about all this writing?" at the beginning of the marvelous 1922 poem "Young Love"?

67. Do you know what I mean when I say "The Love Song of J. Alfred Prufrock" is to T. S. Eliot what "The Negro Speaks of Rivers" is to Langston Hughes?

68. Where do we put Jean Toomer?

69. Would you say Langston Hughes is more popular but Jean Toomer is more modernist, or would you say Hughes is more social but Toomer is more pastoral?

70. Who knows the story of Langston Hughes and Gwendolyn Brooks running around Chicago during its Harlem Renaissance–adjacent Bronzeville Renaissance?

71. Which is most critical: a. T. S. Eliot's "Tradition and the Individual Talent," b. Marianne Moore's *Idiosyncrasy & Technique,* or c. Hart Crane's "General Aims and Theories"?

72. Who understands *The Bridge* by Hart Crane?

73. How many poets with inherently poetic names can you name?

74. Wouldn't it be great if the filmmaker Terrence Malick filmed an episode of poetic history based on the lush, humid imagery in Jean Toomer's novel *Cane*?

75. Who can forget a name like Sterling Brown?

End of Twentieth Century Examination, Part III?

A Lucille Clifton-Inspired Sterling Brown Teaching Fable

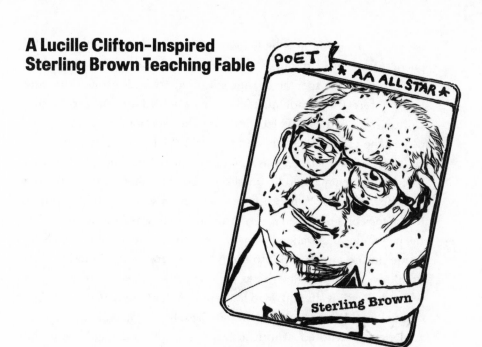

POET
★ AA ALL STAR ★
Sterling Brown

Part I

"Let America be America again." Sterling Brown began addressing the aspiring, emerging, and deluded Black student poets of his literary salon some unspecified evening in the District of Columbia. He spoke at the frequency of commandments given by a poet lord in command of the language of his kidnappers. His lesson plan unfolded again and again between 1926 and 1968 as he hunted for the true poets, dormant and emergent. Ster' Brown he was called by the trees and stars, because the moles on his face branched into stars over time. "When Hughes says, 'Let it be the dream it used to be,'" asked the Stare—the name accorded him by students struck dumb as proverbial deer—"does he refer to the childhood of America, or does he refer to the boy he was?" He shares a photograph of Langston Hughes reading the poem over his typewriter. Then a photo of Hughes at twelve. Professor Brown asked members of the literary salon to repeat to themselves, "America never was America to me," until reaching a frequency that made them shake or vibrate. He uttered his command most encouragingly; still, some of the young poets of the salon faded immediately into the subject of the poem. Others said the lines aloud along with Brown, nodding their heads, but let the spell go as they scattered home. Most ceased being poets before they graduated. Though Brown's best student, Lucille Clifton, dropped out of Howard after her sophomore year, she repeated the refrain when she returned to Buffalo to become a mother and wife: "America never was America to me." She immediately understood a frequency could be unlocked, allowing listeners to retune the lines of the poem. "America never was America to me" with a punch to *America* or a punch to *never.* "America never was America to me" in the beginning and gradually with variety. "America never was America to me" in the mirror and into the pillow wherever she found mirrors or pillows in her day. She thinks back on Brown's reading of the poem when she was his student. Had he wept that day? There had been some discussion of Whitman hiding in the poem like a god and slave master. And some anecdote featuring a shirtless, drunk, laughing Hughes the night before Senator Joseph McCarthy's Congress tried him for communism. Hughes thought he would be sent to prison. Brown said he'd never seen him that drunk. In heaven, for my achievements, I aim for the Sterling Brown teaching award.

Part II

Lesson Plan

"Let America Be America Again" continues to generate myriad conversations. Students are asked to encounter it as if entering a house, a shelter of linguistic textures. We grasp the context of the poem very quickly. A smart student detects some mid-twentieth-century vibe emanating from its uncomplicated democratic designations, the frank identifications of workers and races. The poem was published in *Esquire* magazine in 1936, the year Lucille Clifton was born in Buffalo, New York. Students are asked to research the Great Depression. Smart students observe the text does not really date itself. Students are asked to update the poem. We know there may be myriad contexts to a poem, but only a few, sometimes subtle, often emotionally detectable, subtexts. The most heated conversations may come via the poem's subtext. Does such a poem flood your basement with feelings, or does it flood your basement with ideas?

Audiovisuals

On the wall of the salon is a photograph of Langston Hughes and Sterling Brown after a lecture at Howard University in 1957. Students will be aware of the relationship between Brown and Hughes, the one being slightly lighter than the other on his tones, slightly lighter on his toes, and one of slightly lighter complexion. Both poets were born in 1901. Some say the publication of Sterling Brown's classic *Southern Road* in 1932 coincided with the emergence of the Harlem Renaissance. Some say it was Langston Hughes's *The Weary Blues* in 1926 that kick-started the era. Brown taught at Howard University from 1926 to 1969, educating several generations of Black folk. Hughes lived as a poet from 1926 until his death in 1967. The two appear alike at a distance. For general class discussion: Who is a teaching poet, and who is the poet who teaches?

Video

"Lucille Clifton and Sonia Sanchez: Mirrors & Windows"

Filmed October 24, 2001, at the New School, New York, New York. Moderated by Eisa Davis (https://youtu.be/O8aCnU9oArI).

Lucille Clifton on Hughes

"I remember getting a letter from Langston [Hughes], and it came to my father's house, and my father was sitting there. I went by there for something, and my father was sitting there with the letter in his lap looking at me. And he had known this was gonna happen, I'm sure. And he said, 'You got a letter from a communist, what you gon do?' Who's a communist? Stalin? But on the other hand, my father—who was not . . . he was an uneducated kind of man, an interesting human—he'd have me write the notes for him; he sent me, I remember, to school with a note, 'She do not have to pledge to the flag. When it means to her what it means to a white girl, then she may stand.' So I'm thinking, yeah, but, people, I was twelve—you know what I mean."

Lucille Clifton on Brown

"Sterling Brown had a group of writers who met and, now, how he let me be a part of that, I have no clue. But it was Sterling Brown, Owen Dodson, James Baldwin (when he was there), Joe Walker, and me. And I then didn't appreciate it, of course, but later I did; and I have no idea why I was—why he allowed me to be in his presence. That's where I first heard Billie Holiday."

Part III

Undiscovered "Let America Be America Again" Pop Quiz

1. Between which lines does Hughes pause like someone who has forgotten something?

    (A) Between *"Say, who are you that mumbles in the dark?"* and *"And who are you that draws your veil across the stars?"*

    (B) Between *"I am the poor white, fooled and pushed apart"* and *"I am the Negro bearing slavery's scars."*

    (C) Between *"Say, who are you that mumbles"* and *"in the dark?"*

    (D) Between beginning and ending.

2. To what audience is Langston Hughes speaking in "Let America Be America Again"?

    (A) A dozen or so couples in a small Harlem jazz club owned by a friend of Sterling Brown.

    (B) Owen Dodson, Alain Locke, and the Negro scholars of the day gathered for a conference on "The New Negro," angling for the regard the poet holds for Sterling Brown.

    (C) Skeptical Black college students of Sterling Brown's university amused by the shape of Langston Hughes's head and voice.

    (D) Mostly poets.

3. The best refrain of "Let America Be America Again" exhibits the rhetorical device known as

    (A) shade

    (B) long sigh

    (C) tooth suck

    (D) hiss

4. Which lines were muttered when Langston Hughes drifted off to dreams over a draft of the poem he sent to Sterling Brown?

   (A) "Tangled in an anecdote's endless air of funk, sourpuss, garter belt, of the garden and nightfall . . ."

   (B) "Out of the raconteur and ruling of our debacle, out of the rack and ruin of our gangster death . . ."

   (C) "In every bridesmaid and stoolpigeon, in every fusion turned that's made America the landlady it has become . . ."

   (D) "I am the workhorse sold to the machinist . . ."

5. What was Langston Hughes overheard saying when he visited Sterling Brown's poetry class?

   (A) "I don't need to visit no aquarium, no zoo; I walk around and see people in cages and underwater too."

   (B) "Why do I have such difficulty accepting my own beauty as natural and true?"

   (C) "Nor could your mothers and fathers say truly who you are."

   (D) "A large part of being smart is about knowing when you're wrong."

BONUS: What did you hear Langston Hughes say when he visited class?

POET ★ AA ALL STAR ★

SONIA SANCHEZ

Sonia Sanchez,
Born 1934

To be Sonia Sanchez you must be born in Birmingham, where your mother dies when you are one, where your grandmother dies when you are six, where four Black girls die when you are twenty-nine. Your hair must stutter into the filament of your mind. To be Sonia Sanchez you must be inexplicably resilient, your pigtails must rest on your father's shoulder on the ride to Harlem in 1944. Your hair must be ironed into bangs of decree as you become a Black woman with a degree in political science in 1955. Your bangs must grow into an afro as you teach elementary school while pursuing postgraduate studies & poetry in Greenwich Village. To be Sonia Sanchez your afro must explode into inaugurations of Black studies programs in universities from California to Pennsylvania, & into the lines of *Homecoming* in 1969, triggering a wake of minds. Your hair must be made of a fiber that makes you both mother & father to twin boys & a daughter. On the covers of *Shake Loose My Skin* & *Homegirls & Hand Grenades*, your hair must be the color of Malcolm X's hair upon his return from Mecca. Writing *Does Your House Have Lions?*, your hair must spiral into the locks of a mane. Writing *Wounded in the House of a Friend*, your locks must become the lock of an embrace. Your locks must wind into quotation marks around lines from Gwendolyn Brooks, Louise Bogan, Toni Morrison & Lucille Clifton & into question marks around lines of fire & defense, lines in the sand, chalk lines & headlines. Your locks must lengthen like a long American sentence punctuated by the songs of Black people. Exclamations of Blackness must explode from the filament of your mind.

Michael S. Harper,
Born 1938

Beneath the hat is a brain born in Brooklyn. Beneath the hat is "My Father's Face," "My Mother's Bible." Beneath the hat is Robert Hayden, the Negro Folk Tradition, Providence, the speckled blues-poet-professor-mentor Sterling Brown & the mad-sanctifying-farmer-turned-abolitionist John Brown. Beneath the hat is "The Militance of a Photograph in the Passbook of a Bantu under Detention," which opens with *"Peace is the active presence of Justice"* & details a Black man with pus swaddling his bandages. Beneath the hat is the shape of an oak's trunk laid bare by the homicidal chainsaw of the State. Beneath the hat is Coltrane asleep on a train, dreaming the names of trees, between New York & Philly. Beneath the hat is "MSH." Beneath the hat is all of

"History as Apple Tree," "History as Polka Dots & Moonbeams," "History as Diabolical Materialism." Beneath the hat is the ghost of the brother who died in a motorcycle accident. Beneath the hat is a church of four Black girls blown up in Alabama, a net holding five hundred Middle Passage Blacks underwater in Charleston harbor. Cries & song lines spill from a tenor tethered to the gut of a Black man playing on a warped record playing on a warped record player beneath the hat. Beneath the hat is "American History," "Bigger's Blues," "Elvin's Blues," "Martin's Blues," a Black man's view of suffering, a Black man's view of beauty, a Black man's view of faith. Beneath the hat is a place a Black man can place a few small apples for his children. Beneath the hat is the oily, salty smell clinging to the skin of the apples when the children eat them.

Barbara Chase-Riboud,
Born 1939

Barbara Chase-Riboud was one of the first seven-year-olds, if not the first, to win a sculpture prize in the adult evening classes of the Fletcher Academy in Philadelphia. Barbara Chase-Riboud was one of the first sixteen-year-old women, if not the first, to show work in the collection of the Museum of Modern Art. Barbara Chase-Riboud was one of the first, if not the first, to sell a bronze sculpture on exhibit at the Spoleto Festival of Two Worlds to Ben Shahn, one of her heroes. In 1978, when Barbara Chase-Riboud discovered the story of Sally Hemings & Thomas Jefferson, Toni Morrison, who was her poetry editor at Random House, said, "You have been talking about this woman for a year. Why don't you just write it yourself?" Barbara Chase-Riboud did so. Barbara Chase-Riboud wrote a poem about the brief affair between Anna Akhmatova & Amedeo Modigliani. In 1988, *Portrait of a Nude Woman as Cleopatra* won the Carl Sandburg Poetry Prize. Barbara Chase-Riboud, not Romare Bearden, was the first artist to appear on the cover of *Ebony* magazine. In 1996, Barbara Chase-Riboud received a knighthood in arts & letters in France. Barbara Chase-Riboud was one of the first people, if not the first, to argue with photographer René Burri in the Valley of the Kings about crossing the Nile on the last boat. Barbara Chase-Riboud knows *Every Time a Knot Is Undone, a God Is Released*. Barbara Chase-Riboud made a sculpture of a beautiful small Greek vase when she was seven years old!

Intro: *SOS: Poems 1961-2013*, Works by Amiri Baraka

Amiri Baraka was old for quite a long time. Amiri Baraka was young for quite a long time. Each of these statements is true, or as quickly becomes evident in *SOS: Poems 1961–2013*, each is as contradictory as the late poet himself, the perennial wise man and wiseass. The collection, if one skims it, yields Baraka's oft-noted inflections and influences: the reeling spontaneity of the Beats, the avant-garde scaffolding of the Black Mountain School, and especially the swaggering cadences of African American vernacular. (I'd include the influence of Black Arts poetics had he not been the movement's chief chef and cultivator.) A closer examination reveals Baraka was also very consistent over the collection's fifty-two-year span. Not just in his attention to Black musical, cultural, and political lore, but in his philosophical leanings. Religion, for example, is a recurring antagonism in the poems—the launchpad from which he targets dogma, doctrine, and duplicity: groupthinkery. (Before dropping out of college, he majored in philosophy and religion.) Titles across the collected poems highlight his heckling appraisals: "Black Dada Nihilismus," "When We'll Worship Jesus," "Heathens," "Why It's Quiet in Some Churches."

SOS: Poems 1961–2013 is also relentlessly irreverent. Baraka often seems akin to a voodoo doctor smiling as he needles American social order. No one is safe from his provocations, puns, and put-downs: not "Tom Ass Clarence," nor "Rush Limp Balls"; not whites, not Blacks, not rich, not poor, and certainly not stupid. In "A Poem for Deep Thinkers" he chastises writers petrified by craft: "the statue graveyard where Ralph Ellison sits biting his banjo / strings retightening his instrument for the millionth time before / playing the star-spangled banner." The poems live by every trickster-comedian's credo: *You can say whatever you want as long as it's funny.* Still, it is painful to acknowledge instances the mockery is, as Baraka later apologetically admitted, "wrongheaded." We could add bilious, reckless, embarrassing. The aspersions and epithets are indefensible, but no serious reader of Baraka's poems would characterize his oeuvre as fundamentally malevolent. The early work reveals a poet exploring the psychology of not only being African American, but of being a being *being.* "An Agony. As Now" begins, "I am inside someone / who hates me. I look / out from his eyes," and ends, "It is a human love, I live inside. . . . It burns the thing / inside it. And that thing / screams." After *The Dead Lecturer,* the contemplative musing of poems like "An Agony. As Now" and the wonderful "Footnote to a Pretentious Book" gives way to the public, polemical speech of cultural and political activism. SOS becomes, for better or/and worse, a signal of blunt urgency.

Whether one views *SOS: Poems 1961–2013* as the work of a bully or prophet, Cassius or Cassandra, this is undeniably the work of the kind of poet we will not see again; one of the last of the twentieth century's literary lions. His peers among the New York School poets, the Beats, the Black Mountain, and Black Arts have legions of adherents and acolytes. Amiri Baraka was inimitable. This momentous collection exhibits his abiding resistance to almost everything, but subversiveness.

TWENTIETH CENTURY EXAMINATION

Part IV: How Should We Go About Awarding Gwendolyn Brooks a Posthumous Nobel Prize in Literature?

1950

Gwendolyn Brooks becomes the first African American writer to win a Pulitzer Prize

1953

Lawrence Ferlinghetti and Peter Martin open City Lights Bookstore in San Francisco

Langston Hughes called before Senator Joseph McCarthy and the House Committee on Un-American Activities (HCUA)

James Baldwin publishes *Go Tell It on the Mountain*

1954

Brown v. Board of Education: US Supreme Court rules segregation in public schools unconstitutional

1955

Emmett Till abducted, tortured, and lynched in Mississippi

1957

Allen Ginsberg's "Howl" wins in a highly publicized obscenity trial

1959

Robert Lowell publishes *Life Studies*

Motown founded

James Baldwin
Musing on You?

Allen Ginsberg
Musing on Freedom of Speech?

The American Muse of Destruction
Eating His Children?

Gwendolyn Brooks Musing on Her People?

Robert Lowell
Musing on *Life Studies*?

Ted Joans
Musing on Jazz Music?

76. Do the words *poetry* and *politics* constitute a portmanteau of *poetics*?

77. Can you remember what happened when Robert Frost won his fourth Pulitzer Prize for Poetry in 1943?

78. In what year did FDR begin his fourth term as president?

79. Am I the only one who feels that Gertrude Stein remains one of the most overlooked and undervalued poets in the American literary canon; that she is still under-taught and under-thought despite becoming more original and more pertinent and prescient with each passing year?

80. Did you know Margaret Walker was a Yale Younger Poets Prize winner in 1942 for *For My People*?

81. Does Gwendolyn Brooks, who published her landmark debut in 1945, overshadow Margaret Walker because we have overlooked Walker or because Walker has a different talent?

82. Would Walker have produced more if she'd had more support?

83. You ever wonder why Missouri native T. S. Eliot spoke with a British accent?

84. Don't we want a movie about hairy Gerald Stern and wild-eyed Jack Gilbert running around Pittsburgh and Paris between wars?

85. Is it possible to think of anything in the 1940s without thinking of the two atomic bombs the United States of America dropped on Japan?

86. Do you think reading poems or writing poems is the better practice?

87. Would you agree it's possible to be both enlightened and in the dark?

88. Who said "to write poetry after Auschwitz is barbaric"?

89. Is it only line breaks that make poets different from other writers?

90. Did you know the same year Gwendolyn Brooks became the first Black writer to win a Pulitzer Prize, an updated *Oxford Book of American Verse* was published with no Black poets?

91. Shouldn't James Baldwin's *Go Tell It on the Mountain* be read by everyone?

92. Who should play Langston Hughes in the Langston Hughes movie, someone the color of sunset or someone the color of rum cake?

93. Is Robert Lowell the quintessential poet of the prewar-to-postwar era?

94. Is Robert Lowell or Wallace Stevens the whitest poet in the canon?

95. Is it possible the soul of Dylan Thomas was transferred to Mark Doty, who was born in the year of Thomas's death?

96. Can you remember what happened when James Wright won the Yale Younger Poets Prize for *The Green Wall* in 1956?

97. Who remembers that Lawrence Ferlinghetti was arrested for publishing Allen Ginsberg's "Howl"?

98. What part should intent play in determining the meaning of a poem?

End of Twentieth Century Examination, Part IV?

Toi Derricotte,
Born 1941

Toi Derricotte was born in Michigan in the first year of the Second World War to a Duke Ellington–toned undertaker from Kentucky & a Creole Louisiana beauty Joe Louis himself described as a knockout. Here are some of Derricotte's gifts to people who live by poems: An openness found nowhere else in American poetry, except maybe in the way Jean Toomer describes flowers in a storm. A humor that can be wired as John Berryman's *Dream Songs* or weird as Bob Kaufman's sardines. A daughter of undertaker & overseer, of Duke & Lady Day, of Brooks & Hayden; a niece to Lorde & Clifton; a sister to Eady & Olds; queen of the evening mothering us Black orphan poets. A stamina for tenderness & the cost of paying attention. A mirror on the self from Detroit to "Clitoris": a way to speak what is witnessed.

Lorenzo Thomas,
Born 1944

[BROKEN ABECEDARIAN LORENZO CENTO]

A hurricane is swirling in the gulf all Americans are losing. All silence says
music will follow because it is conceived as a tonal evocation. Bloodless
hands glowing. Can you read my gestures? Come on with the foliage.
Eating your petals in the afternoon I wanted to be so fancy. Given choices standing in the street. Grateful. Here is no redly opulent Cossack. No
painted Trinity. History is still ephemera. I am trying to make my songs.
I'd rather take flying lessons. If any man were willing to change places I
gather light. I know where I belong. It's not that I've grown blind. It was
when neon was no longer available. I was born a speck of sand. John
Donne would think of an island knowing I will not sleep tonight. Life's not
light with a veil of dust. Love fills its absences with doubt. Morning morn-

ing Sunday. Night just keeps on arriving. O excellent night. One person amplified. One hundred only fit now. Part of it thought up in the silence. Say justice speaks so she contends with clouds of fortune. Since you are my lover I sit erect in an ordinary chair. Sometimes I'm saying I love you. That will not make these lyrics more beautiful. The idle boys are waiting in the park. The land was there before us. There are no gospel singers. There is a place beyond the reach. The song light sparkles. The vipers advance this useless clairvoyance to a lotus. Tonight, I count my sins. We are traveling to and forth on the sound. What shines is your Black body when you are alive. You cannot sleep. You have this world and others.

(Based on *The Collected Poems of Lorenzo Thomas*, index of first lines)

Ai,
Born 1947

Ai kept cats because she could be lonely. Ai rode the feathers of a comet into the world. Wearing a wedding dress, Ai buried Mama in a wedding dress & delivered her eulogy crying in a dream. Ai could be Japanese, Choctaw-Chickasaw & Black because of a streetcar stop. Ai could be Irish, Southern Cheyenne, Comanche & Black. Ai was the child of a scandalous affair. Ai was Tuscan at a crossroads. Ai was Florence Anthony in Texas. Carolyn Wright said Ai bought a turquoise necklace. Ai was a moonstone stained with the twilight of June in Oklahoma. Ai was disguised as a poem in the pocket of a Catholic school uniform in California. Ai could be Miguel Hernández, Gabriel García Márquez. Ai could be César Vallejo predicting death in "Black

Stone on a White Stone." Ai could be Yasunari Kawabata, "Talking to His Reflection in a Shallow Pond." In the blues, the singer is always guilty; in opera, there's often murder in the song. Wearing a kimono, Ai buried her father wearing a kimono & delivered his eulogy crying in a dream. "I absorb you through my skin." It's not that Ai wouldn't buy you a tiara because she was mean; she wouldn't buy it for you because she watched her money carefully. Ai wrote *Cruelty* in 1973 & *Sin* in '86. Ai wrote *Fate* in 1991 & *Greed* in '93. Ai said Jesus "walked on his mother's body to be the King of Heaven." Ai could be the Blackest soul in the Bible, the bride of the prophet, the least-remembered disciple. Ai lived it. Ai could be within earshot of a catcall or eyeballing another poet's boondoggle. Bromides pretend to be wise. Ai on a shoebox on the brown leather high-back chair. Ai on a cracked glass on a cluttered counter. Ai on earth. Ai on a magic carpet. Ai parked an old maroon Ford in a field outside El Reno. Ai was wing up on the sideboard of the old car. Ai was sidesaddle to the headstrong odor of a ghost. "I'm on my way to work." "When you run off, I start after you."

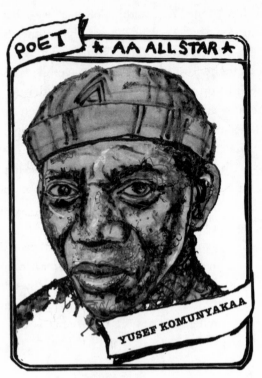

Yusef Komunyakaa,
Born 1947

One glimpses what one did not know" "We know the men from women by the colors they wear" "He knows 'We Shall Overcome' & anthems of the flower children" "& the Angel knows defeat" "But I know when the question flew Into my head" "I need to know if iron tastes like laudanum Or a woman" "These ghosts know the power of suggestion is more than body language" "There's a pain inside of me, but I don't know where" "I know laughter can rip stitches, & deeds come undone in the middle of a dance" "I know all seven songs of the sparrow" "I mean, I also know something about night riders & catgut. Yeah, honey, I know something about talking with ghosts" "I've known of secret graves guarded by the night owl in oak & poplar" "I know all the monsters lurking in Lord Byron's verses" "I know, I also said I'd kiss the devil" "I know time opens an apple seed to find a worm" "I know the scent of belladonna" "I know hearsay can undo a kingdom" "I, too, know my Hopkins (Lightnin' & Gerard Manley)" "I know a dried-up riverbed & extinct animals live in your nightmares" "& now I know why I'd rather die a poet than a warrior, tattoo & tomahawk"

*Twenty Years of Knowing: *An Everyday Mojo Songs of Earth* Cento

Everyday Mojo Letters to Yusef

"THE NEW LAW RIDING A TABLECLOTH"
Alternate title: "How Yusef Got North"

Start of the Sixteenth Draft of an Excessively Worded Document Titled "Everyday Mojo Letters to Yusef"

Dear Yusef, I was thinking I'd write about your star in the genre of the Black Jazz Poet, but I keep changing what I mean by *Black* and *Jazz* and *Poet*. Such words come boxed in metaphor. Ken Burns, for example, said the word *jazz* was derived from the scent of jasmine on prostitutes when Louis Armstrong was a boy in New Orleans. The poetry of a Black man gets romanticized and boxed in the same way. The difference between the jazz of Louis Armstrong and the jazz of Miles Davis says how useless it can be to describe the spirit of jazz or Blackness or manhood. To call you a Black jazz poet is to call you an elusive walking metaphor. Was it John Coltrane who said, "I don't play jazz; I play John Coltrane"? You are not simply writing "jazz poems" at this point; you are writing "Yusef Komunyakaa." Duke Ellington was clearly playing Duke Ellington. "Jazz has always been a man telling the truth about himself," Quincy Jones said. (A Black woman can be heard saying, *That might be why jazz is dying, Quincy.*) Gordon Parks simply said jazz was inherently elusive: "The meaning of it is as evasive as silence." I love Gordon Parks.

Like *jazz*, the word *mojo* is one of those words that got its roots clipped or crisscrossed during the Middle Passage. I read somewhere it can be traced back to the West African medicine man. The root doctor carrying cures for the body in a mojo hand. I know the griot's gris-gris wards off griefs and ghosts. In the first poem in *Everyday Mojo Songs of Earth*, "A World of Daughters," you write, "One glimpses what one did not know," and the sense echoes across the pages. What does it mean to *know* in *Everyday Mojo Songs of Earth*? It sounds less fixed than "knowledge." It's the kind of "knowing" that is glimpsed; it is insistent and fixed as a refrain. "A World of Daughters" makes me think of something you wrote about "Requiem," the last poem of the book, on the Poetry Society of America website: "I knew I wanted to attempt to capture a continuous motion, looping and winding, dredging up and letting go."

Starting with new poems that lead back to older poems make any reading of a selected poems "a continuous motion." For example, the intimate and allegorical pitch of "A World of Daughters" returns later in "Requiem." Or how the book feels wonderfully framed in prayer when I read "A Prayer for Workers" in the new poems and later return to "Prayer" in *The Emperor of Water Clocks* (2015). The collection is also framed by those ghazals, "The Mountain" and "Ghazal, after Ferguson." In my most perfect world there would be a forthcoming collection of Yusefian jazz ghazals.

Mojo Letter after Erik Satie's Instructions for Playing *"Gnossienne* No. 3"

Dear Yusef, after Ed asked me to write about this new book, I dug out an interview we did in New York in the spring of 2002. I remember trying to get you to say things you hadn't said before about your influences, your ambitions, yourself. I have been circling back to one of my questions:

> In *Blue Notes* you said, "It is difficult for me to write about things in my life that are very private, but I feel I am constantly moving closer to my personal terrain, to the idea of trying to get underneath who I am." What are you doing to get closer to this more private terrain, and how do you draw the line between the Private and the Public, as a poet?

You slyly did not answer the question. I also dug out a brief, medio-cre review of *Talking Dirty to the Gods* (2000) I wrote for the *Xavier Review*. I was so embarrassed when I read it, I decided to write you a letter of apology. I shuddered at my critiques of what I called your "leaps of obscurity" in the book. The tiny eyes of a young poet. Icarus critiquing the wings of Daedalus just before takeoff. I've learned to embrace the confusion I sometimes experience inside a poem. (Our young poets will ask for an example, and I will say, "Find your own damn example of confusion.")

I've spent the last two months poking at Erik Satie's "*Gnossienne* No. 3" between poking around your poems. Satie's coinage of the word *gnossienne* is rooted in *gnosis*, the Greek word for "knowledge." Satie's use of the word is not incidental to his interest in gnosticism, but the original *gnosis* suggests the kind of circular, lyric, *open* knowledge that helps me think about you.

Everyday Mojo Songs of Earth got me thinking about the continuous motion between learning and knowing. I've learned to look forward to the things I don't know—the room left inside a Yusef poem—the way I look forward to the room Satie leaves me in his compositions. His first and third *Gnossiennes* share similar motifs and patterns but are written without bar lines or time signatures. The third is easiest, so I figured learning it would make learning the first easier. The waltz of the left hand is a dressed-up kind of blues minimalism. A "dressed-up kind of blues" works as a *jazz* definition sometimes. Satie, a famously weird dude, was, I suppose, afraid folks would not get the mysteries/obscuri-ties of the *Gnossiennes*. He left a set of instructions specific to playing each piece. For "*Gnossienne* No. 1," he advises the player to "wonder about yourself." I haven't started learning that one yet. For "*Gnossienne* No. 3," he advises the player to "counsel yourself cautiously," and "be clairvoyant," "alone for a second," "Very Lost." I am still learning to feel clairvoyantly self-counseled in poems.

I don't believe we have ever actually talked about poems or poetry in all our years of hanging out. For our first poetry conference nearly twenty-five years ago, we listened to jazz with the wiry widow of an abstract expressionist amid the kayaks and canoes she rowed across

Provincetown. Listening to music with you and Pat is on my list of top ten ecstatic life memories. Listening was feedback. You, Larry, Radi, and me listening to live jazz at the Candlelight Lounge is also somewhere on that as-yet-unpenned list.

Readers will not be wrong, exactly, to highlight the presence of jazz in your book, but "The Candlelight Lounge" is as concerned with community as it is with music: "Faces in semi-dark cluster around a solo." Readers will not be any more wrong to highlight the presence of jazz in your poems than they would be to highlight the presence of jazz in the poetry of Michael S. Harper or Al Young. Y'all are as uniquely oriented—or about as harmonic in your love of jazz—as a room of uncles debating which song should be played at the family reunion. Poems like "The Candlelight Lounge" measure the impact of the music as much as they track its construction. *Talking Dirty to the Gods* marks the transition to a kind of poem that can invoke jazz poetics with or without concerning itself with jazz as a subject. I could write about you and the genre of the Jazz Poet, but you keep changing what *jazz* means.

Mojo Letter Cannibalized by a Failed Unboxing Video Script for *Everyday Mojo Songs of Earth*

On YouTube you can find a whole genre of these videos of people unboxing new stuff. I've seen a few smartphone unboxings, and a few sneaker unboxings, an unboxing of a compact automobile. I watched a few before writing my own unboxing script. The book arrives in a real box. "You want to come at it from as many angles as possible," I say, cutting into the cardboard where it is held by tape. Inside the book inside the box, I begin removing lines of poems and holding them up to the camera. The lines echo with innuendo and throw shadows. The lines evaporating at the mouth. "Yeah, honey, I know something about talking with ghosts." Everything in the box is useful. Make something with the box. Even if you have no glue and scissors, you can turn it into a legible surface or fortress or sculpture. Throw nothing away. "Do not necessarily subscribe," I say as I lower myself into the box of poems. I begin to hear sideways piano. Sometimes I will just sit and read Komunyakaa poems out loud in the unboxing video. These poems make a vintage entrance and provide vibrant everyday interactions. Inside the book inside the box, find poems never before seen by readers old and new. Storms, crows, gunmetal drones, shouts, circadian incantations, mantras of healing expand in the box. The liberty and music of musing and muscling mischief out of melancholy are packed into the box. "Great Ooga-Booga" almost rhymes with *didgeridoo*. Inside the box, there's a room where belladonna and jasmine mingle on a humid afternoon in New Orleans. "There's a pain inside of me, but I don't know where." "I know laughter can rip stitches, & deeds come undone in the middle of a dance." "I know all seven songs of the sparrow." Inside the box all the lost brothers, sons, and nephews are not lost. "The mojo is a talisman and practice, a noun and action, and you, Reader," I say, shouting up from inside the box, "are privy to the everyday mojo songs of a psychic blues historian like Zora Neale Hurston and Sterling Brown. Yusef Komunyakaa is one of those fortune-tellers born of soothsayers who raise griots who live as teachers," I say, vanishing between the lines.

Mojo Letter in the Spirit of the Young Poet's Letter to Rilke

"Go into yourself," Rainer Maria Rilke advises the military cadet and aspiring young poet Franz Kappus in *Letters to a Young Poet*. (I don't know if that's a thing a real poet needs to hear. It's incredibly useful for a reader, though: the instruction to "go into yourself" as you read.) There is no wrong way into the self. Kappus was a nineteen-year-old at the time he wrote Rilke, who was himself twenty-seven. The exchange might be more like undergraduate student to graduate student than mentee to mentor were we not talking about Rilke. The other day I was shocked when one of our well-read young poets did not know your poem "Venus's-flytraps." That should be standard Komunyakaa canon by now. I dropped into your baritone: "I am five wading out into deep sunny grass." I played a couple recordings I have of you reading the poem. I directed him to my Vimeo bootleg mash-up of you reading the poem over the railroad scene in Andrei Tarkovsky's *Stalker* and scenes from *Kirikou and the Sorceress*. Fanatic-fan-in-a-pandemic shit. I know almost no body of work better than I know yours. Or it may be better to say no body of work is more deeply in my blood than yours.

I remember when I was a young poet hearing your name for the first time. When I was nineteen or twenty, poet Judson Mitcham said what sounded like a foreign spell with a magical drawl. I knew only the poems of Black poets I found in literature anthologies when I was in college. Gwendolyn Brooks, Robert Hayden, Etheridge Knight, Amiri Baraka, Audre Lorde. I don't even think Rita Dove or Lucille Clifton were in some of those textbooks yet. In 1991 when Mitcham visited my tiny, maybe-two-thousand-student-bodied campus in Hartsville, South Carolina, I got to sit with him and talk poems. At some point he wrote your name in fine southern cursive on a torn slip of paper. Not long after that, I bought my first poetry book, Jorie Graham's 1990 edition of *The Best American Poetry*, because I spotted you beside "Facing It." That poem rearranged my mind. (I think actually *Good Night, Willie Lee* was the first poetry book I bought, when I was fifteen, but it was because I had a crush on Alice Walker, not because of those very good poems. Someone should do a retrospective of Walker's poetry.)

My debates with my pal Renegade over *the* key Komunyakaa poem always include "Facing It," "Venus's-flytraps," "Anodyne." Your new book only makes the debates more impossible to resolve. And the poem "Fortress" is reason enough to reread everything I've read before. How did I miss that poem? I shudder to think how much beauty is covered by blind spots. "Fortress" feels like some of the poems from *Magic City* carved down to nectar. When you write, "I see the back door / of that house close to the slow creek / where a drunken, angry man stumbles / across the threshold every Friday," the father reaching for a can of Jax at the opening of "My Father's Love Letters" echoes in my heart. You write, "I see forgiveness, unbearable twilight, / & these two big hands know too much / about nail & hammer." Hands open and reach across your poems. I could have found enough references to hands here for another mojo hand cento, but I stopped myself.

The last of my questions during that 2002 interview was, "When you think about being fifteen years old, what do you remember being obsessed with?" You answered, "Strangely enough, I was obsessed with building a greenhouse. I had drawn up all these elaborate plans and I thought that's what I would really do." Rilke tells the young poet to find his reason for writing: "Confess to yourself whether you would have to die if you were forbidden to write." You say late in the book, "Now I know why I'd rather die a poet than a warrior, tattoo & tomahawk."

Mojo Letter in the Spirit of Vincent van Gogh's Letters to Theo

The distance between Van Gogh in Paris and the asylum in Arles may be in no way comparable to the distance between New Orleans and Bogalusa to the few souls on the planet to visit all four. Possibly only Yusef Komunyakaa has seen and said more about such worlds. All who dare summarize a poem must then be forced to summarize Thelonious Monk, *Starry Night*, joy and shame. One of the plantations on the outskirts of a town somewhere has been converted into a spa of psychiatric poetics. But *psychiatric*, it seems, is metaphor for nightglow, psychokinetic, audiovisual sentences where what is seen and said of the world is music. The ghost of Professor Longhair plays a legless piano in a Van Gogh painting above the chameleon couch where the doctor's patients rest their eyes. The doctor has the patients read Komunyakaa poems as answers to their plights. All who dare summarize a painting must then be forced to summarize mojo, vibrato, bravado, taste. I love the singing double-talk between "Ignis Fatuus" and "Fata Morgana," the blue dementia of Orpheus at the gate between worlds. The photographs of Van Gogh's paintings projected on the walls of a museum somewhere in the distant future or far back as the cave of Plato, let us remember, are not the painter's paintings. I shudder to think how much beauty is covered by blind spots. With my eyes closed, below the painting, talking to the doctor, I begin to hear sideways piano. Music emanates from the painting when I look at it with my eyes closed. The ghost of Professor Longhair plays piano on the floor in a museum with walls covered in projections of Van Gogh's colored brushstrokes. The great Bogalusa poet has returned to town. A poem arrives every time Yusef Komunyakaa comes round.

Mojo Letter in the Spirit of James Baldwin's Letter to His Nephew

Dear Yusef, for the last month I have been circling back to the spirit of James Baldwin writing his fifteen-year-old nephew and namesake in 1962. Weren't you around fifteen in 1962 too? You talked about discovering Baldwin as a teenager during our interview in 2002. At the time I wondered whether those private essays in your files and yellow writing pads would ever see the light of day. They need not. The poems themselves are a response to the unspeakable grief shadowing these years. Poetry makes every day some kind of song. I am a witness. I imagine you a Black fifteen-year-old greenhouse dreamer reading Baldwin's letter to his namesake in the Bogalusa library. He might as well have been speaking to you. My father, James, was born four years after you. I guess you already know the name James is common among Black folks of a certain generation. You might be part of the baby boomer generation had you grown up middle class, safe, and white. Your generation heard word of Emmett Till's murder in real time. Baldwin means to instill in the younger James a sense of self rooted in the tangled realities/histories/impulses of America. He articulates, to my mind, an unprecedented expression of love for you in 1962. There are few other literary expressions of a Black man's love of another Black man, and most of those also are found in the writing of Baldwin. (I have been reading you in the months following the riot of racists who raised a Confederate flag inside the Capitol. I mean, who could have imagined it? [Other than Octavia Butler, that is.] The riot may have surpassed our ability to imagine how much white people can get away with in this country.) The year 1962 is also when Sonny Rollins released *The Bridge*. Do you know the story of his twelve to fifteen hours of practice a day on the Williamsburg Bridge? The title track reminds me of a manic, possibly panicked, lyrically frantic Bird accompanied by drummer, double bass, and Djangoistic guitarist. It's terrific, so live. Then it's followed by this mellow "God Bless the Child." Sometimes music is as close as we can get to prayer.

Does the nephew write his uncle back? Was his name even really James? I could find nothing about him online. I imagine the Jameses pausing on the bridge where Rollins plays. "You come from a long line of great poets," Baldwin says in the letter. You are the kind of great poet he means, Yusef. You cross the bridge carrying the song.

Mojo Letter in the Spirit of the Letter to Bob Kaufman by Yusef Komunyakaa

Inside the box my father's father's name waits to be found in a marvel of marble and stone erected inside your baritone warble. Emily Dickinson knew every poem is a letter to someone because every letter is a poem and said so because she had blackbirds for eyeballs. I say she was reborn as Bob Kaufman. The cries of Dickinson when she was alive sounded like hymns because the only songs she knew came from the Bible, whereas the cries of Kaufman continue to reverberate as silence. Two or three years before Kaufman transforms again, someone drives him home to New Orleans for a final passage of respects, voodoo, and song. I read you as you read him and dance the calinda with yourself like a poet from New Jersey. A house of stairs and shadows where you dream a spell for the root worker. Inside the box the brothers, sons, and nephews of James are not gone. Bob was right next door, God as my witness, floating two or three inches from the floor as he improvised a poem.

TWENTIETH CENTURY EXAMINATION

Part V: How Old Is Contemporary Poetry?

1960
Donald Allen edits *The New American Poetry*

1963
Civil Rights March on Washington

John F. Kennedy is assassinated

Sylvia Plath's suicide

James Baldwin publishes his essay "The Fire Next Time"

1965–73
The Vietnam War

1965
Malcolm X is assassinated

Amiri Baraka moves to Harlem and founds the Black Arts Repertory Theater/School

1968
Martin Luther King Jr. is assassinated

Robert F. Kennedy is assassinated

1969
Stonewall riots in New York City

John Berryman publishes *The Dream Songs*

Elizabeth Bishop
Musing on *Questions of Travel*?

Sylvia Plath
Musing on Lines of Existence?

The American Muse of Destruction
with Another Prisoner of War?

Lucille Clifton
Musing on Blackness?

Frank O'Hara
Musing on Personality?

The Muse of Henry Dumas
Haunting the wake of Henry Dumas?

99. Do you think Frank O'Hara was somewhere reading from *Lunch Poems* when some Black students were attacked for sitting at a Woolworth's lunch counter?

100. How about two actors play LeRoi Jones and Amiri Baraka discussing anti-Semitism in an episode of a less comedic season of poetic history set in the 1960s?

101. Is it possible to think of anything in the 1950s without thinking of the murder of Emmett Till in 1955?

102. Does Emmett Till or Rosa Parks trigger the Civil Rights Movement?

103. Did you know President John F. Kennedy was assassinated in the same year James Baldwin published *The Fire Next Time*?

104. What would constitute a perfect poem for you?

105. Who kept loving Sylvia Plath and Jimi Hendrix after high school, college, and middle age?

106. Who, in general, lives longer, painters or poets?

107. What is Time?

108. What are (your) ecopoetics?

109. Did you know Lucille Clifton went to Howard University with Amiri Baraka when he was known as LeRoi Jones?

110. If the poet representative of the last American century is, like the century, a mess of experiments, contradictions, and conviction, isn't Baraka a pretty good representative poet?

111. How about a vision of the American poet starring a mother (Lucille Clifton) who writes poems while raising her six children in Maryland in the 1970s?

112. Can you believe that Baraka's 1968 anthology of Afro-American writing, *Black Fire*, featured essays by John Henrik Clarke and Harold Cruse and poems by Sun Ra, David Henderson, A. B. Spellman, Sonia Sanchez, Henry Dumas, Jay Wright, Stanley Crouch, Lorenzo Thomas, and Victor Hernández Cruz, but did not include poems by Lucille Clifton, Gwendolyn Brooks, Robert Hayden, Bob Kaufman, Etheridge Knight, or Audre Lorde?

113. What do you think of Audre Lorde's "Power"?

114. Have you ever read "Those Winter Sundays" and wondered what happened to the mother in the poem?

115. Have you ever met anyone familiar with the poems of Allen Ginsberg's father, Louis Ginsberg?

116. If you write a poem like "Howl," do you really need to write anything else?

117. Is "Howl" an example of a poem that actually changed things?

118. When you write a poem, what does it teach you about the past?

119. Did you know Ginsberg reads the entirety of his poem "When the Light Appears" in the song "When the Light Appears Boy" on the album *When I Was Born for the 7th Time*, released by Cornershop in 1997, the year of Ginsberg's death?

120. Did you know that was his voice on "Ghetto Defendant" by The Clash ("Starved in metropolis / Hooked on necropolis / Addict of metropolis / Do the worm on the acropolis / Slamdance the cosmopolis / Enlighten the populace . . .")?

121. Do you sort of think of the Beat poets in the same way you think of the Grateful Dead, with members wandering around like several hairy, high Walt Whitmans?

122. Couldn't we debate whether Robert Lowell or Ginsberg is more confessional?

123. Is it true Bob Kaufman took a vow of silence to protest the Vietnam War?

124. Who brings more intimacy and toughness to poetry than Lucille Clifton?

125. What if every day you ask poetry of yourself?

End of Twentieth Century Examination, Part V?

James Baldwin Cave Canem Keynote, 2017

1.

James Baldwin has received some renewed and long-overdue attention these last years, partly because of the documentary *I Am Not Your
Negro*, and perhaps because of Ta-Nehisi Coates's *Between the World
and Me*. Because we live in a moment of bewildering and familiar civil
struggle, we hear James Baldwin speaking a little bit louder. Of course,
he's always talking to us. Ten or fifteen years ago maybe the same
people who read Audre Lorde and Lucille Clifton to themselves were
closely listening to Baldwin. Six or eight years ago we heard him almost
congratulating us just as we congratulated ourselves for our beautiful
Black president. While some of us asked at that time and still ask today,
"Where the hell did Barack Obama come from?" James Baldwin was
talking about him and that moment—years ago. There's a scene in *I Am
Not Your Negro* where Baldwin responds to Bobby Kennedy's comment
that a Negro could be president of the United States in about forty
years. It was 1968. Baldwin rolls his eyes when he mentions Kennedy's
comments in the documentary. It is not that he can't imagine a Negro
president; it's that he can't believe the vanity of white folk. Baldwin
writes about it in that second essay in *The Fire Next Time*. "Letter from

a Region in My Mind" is a masterpiece. It appeared in *The New Yorker* in November of 1962. He writes:

> White Americans find it as difficult as white people else-where do to divest themselves of the notion that they are in possession of some intrinsic value that Black people need, or want. And this assumption—which, for example, makes the solution to the Negro problem depend on the speed with which Negroes accept and adopt white standards—is revealed in all kinds of striking ways, from Bobby Kennedy's assurance that a Negro can become President in forty years to the unfortunate tone of warm congratulation with which so many liberals address their Negro equals.

No one holds white liberals to account—no other writer lets well-meaning white people have it—like Baldwin. So they don't really know what to do with him. They know they're supposed to like him, because the smart Black people they know like him. But he's too moody for them. He's moody all through the film. Even when he critiques Bobby Kennedy, you can see the devilish delight in him. He's almost teasing him. The mostly white audience I sat with chuckled both times I saw the film. I'm not sure they got why Baldwin was irked. I'm not even sure they got all the implications of the movie's title, *I Am Not Your Negro*. I'm not *whose* Negro? "I am not *white* people's Negro" is not the same as "I am not *Black* people's Negro." It is very likely white people have far fewer definitions of *Negro* than Black people. With Black people *Negro* is not neutral. It is used ironically, euphemistically, dismissively, always in judgment. As in, "He's one of those Negroes who loves to name-drop James Baldwin." As in, "Several Negroes showed up at James Baldwin's funeral."

"Letter from a Region in My Mind" roots much of its insights about class and race in a lovely, near-associative meditation on religion for Black people. Baldwin writes beautifully about growing up in the Black church. "There is no music like that music, no drama like the drama of the saints rejoicing, the sinners moaning, the tambourines racing, and all those voices coming together and crying holy unto the Lord." A core scene in the essay is his visit to the home of Elijah Muhammad, leader of the Nation of Islam at the time. This happened a few years before the assassination of Malcolm X, which is to say the Nation of Islam still had a great deal of credibility and possibility for Black people. Elijah Muhammad had seen Baldwin on a talk show with Brother Malcolm and wanted to meet him. Baldwin loves the dignified ferocity of the brothers and sisters around Elijah Muhammad. He shows a special fondness and respect for Elijah, but that doesn't keep him from knocking down some of the Black Power tenets of the Nation of Islam, number one being the "two nations solution," whereby they called for separate Black territories and properties, and a separate Black economy in America. Baldwin breaks down the logical and logistical problems with such aspirations. He writes, "Power was the subject of the speeches I heard. We were offered, as Nation of Islam doctrine, historical and divine proof that all white people are cursed, and are devils, and are about to be brought down."

Baldwin knows the struggle for power is not the same as the struggle for freedom or justice. Baldwin adds that "white men with far more political power than that possessed by the Nation of Islam movement" have argued with the same blind logic for generations. "If this sentiment is honored when it falls from the lips of Senator Byrd, then there is no reason it should not be honored when it falls from the lips of Malcolm X." It's just a magnificent essay. Near the end his thinking leads him to one of those absolutely mind-blowing Baldwin questions: *"What will happen to all that beauty? . . .* When I sat at Elijah's table and watched the baby, the women, and the men, and we talked about God's—or Allah's—vengeance, I wondered, when that vengeance was achieved, *What will happen to all that beauty then?"*

2.

The Nation of Islam wanted a Black nation because the country felt and still can feel like two nations. A nation of white power needs a nation of people with no power to power it. But it's not just a question of power. A nation of people with no power is still a nation of people who have their own shit. There is still plenty of evidence we live in, at least, two Americas, with separate churches, customs, fashions, TV shows, hair salons. Separate nations naturally require separate anthems: "The Star-Spangled Banner," which is for white America, and "Lift Every Voice and Sing" for the Black people. I have a confession: I'm not really a fan of the Black national anthem.

Anytime I have to sing it I feel something between indifference and an eye roll. You never know when the occasion will arise. Usually, the only person who knows the song by heart is dressed in a dashiki or celebrates Kwanzaa religiously. The lyrics will be printed on the back page of some program celebrating Black achievement. Maybe it's even been sung at a Cave Canem graduation ceremony or two? That's fine. I do sing it. I had to sing it just a few weeks ago at my daughter's high school African American seniors ceremony. The kid who led us in the song had a wonderful voice. But it's not the sort of song you can really throw your heart into. It ain't gospel in the Pentecostal sense. (James Baldwin and Marvin Gaye were raised Pentecostal.) "Lift Every Voice and Sing" is very respectable. Which if someone calls you respectable, that's kind of an insult. It's kind of like calling a Black person a Negro. It's not about the poem written by James Weldon Johnson in 1899 and set to music by his brother, John Rosamond Johnson, in 1905.

Lift every voice and sing,
Till earth and heaven ring,
Ring with the harmonies of Liberty . . .
[Freedom. I believe in singing till you're free.]
Sing a song full of the faith that the dark past has taught us, [Right.]
Sing a song full of the hope that the present has brought us; [Right, I got it, I agree.]
Facing the rising sun of our new day begun,
Let us march on till victory is won.

It's the "till victory is won" part. What does victory look like? Does it look like equality? Technically, that's not victory; that's a draw. Does it look like justice, where you make the oppressor experience a pain similar to that which the oppressor engendered? That just doesn't sound very Christian or Muslim. It's also bad karma. And more important, as Baldwin would tell you, it ain't common sense: you'd just be looking over your shoulder all the time.

What happens to your soul, if the victory is won by vengeance?

I think if someone offered a heartfelt rendition of "Lift Every Voice and Sing" I might be swayed. Maybe Billie or even Jennifer Holliday could sing it as a ballad. I think the song would be transformed if it was sung by a white man. Say, Willie Nelson. It would be as miraculous as hearing a Black man play "The Star-Spangled Banner" one morning at Woodstock before thousands of high, half-naked white people. That wasn't even the first time Hendrix played it. There are several other recordings—which is to say he wasn't just playing it because he was before a bunch of wild white people in Woodstock. Maybe he played it because the nation was at war. And maybe he played it because American leaders—JFK, Malcolm X, MLK, Bobby Kennedy—were being assassinated. And maybe he played it because it's the song we should play when we are in dire straits in this country, "the perilous fight."

It appears on the surface that Cave Canem, an organization for Black poets, represents exactly what the Black nationalists dreamed of: a nation of Black poets of every shade, age, and disposition conspiring poetry. But Cave Canem is not simply a Black nationalist dream. In fact, upon hearing no more than the name Cave Canem, one famous Black nationalist (Amiri Baraka) dismissed it. "Cave Canem? Ain't that Latin?" he said at the Philadelphia Black Writers Conference less than a year after the first Cave Canem retreat in 1996. Why would a Black person name his or her organization after something Latin? Something white? Those who'd attended the retreat tried explaining. Poets Toi Derricotte and Cornelius Eady had been touring the lost city of Pompeii when they visited the house of Tragic Poet. They took as a name the sign posted outside the house of the poet: CAVE CANEM. Its translation is "beware of the dog." Why Cave Canem, why *beware of the dog*? Is the Black poet being guarded by the dog, or is the dog the Black poet? What is Cave Canem? Where do these Black people come from? I believe everything I mean to say to you about the importance of Cave Canem these last twenty years is best said in poetry.

To know Cave Canem you have to know Toi's poems, Cornelius's poems; you need only read a "Cave Canem poem," which I'd simply define as a poem written by a Cave Canem poet; you only need to meet a few Cave Canem poets. You've probably met them. These poets, at all hours of the day as a matter of survival, write poems alone, and then for a week each summer for the last twenty years, they have come together to sing blues and battle songs for extended hours on a diet of metaphor, liquor, spades, and bullshit. These poets wrestle that little serpent of doubt when their poems are rejected. These poets wrestle that little serpent of doubt if their poems are accepted. Where do these people come from? Cave Canem was founded by teachers. Think about that. Toi and Cornelius were teaching at a writers' conference when they began the path that would lead to us. Beyond that and being Black, they had nothing in common beforehand. Toi is the undertaker's daughter out Detroit by way of Louisiana. And Cornelius is the jukebox out of Rochester by way of Florida. Out of these elements they made family. They gathered us: people united by something as ineffable and mysterious and fluid and distinct as Blackness and poetry. A family of half white and high yellow and Asiatic backwoods witch doctors, professors, some students, astrologists, atheists, nationalists, a violinist, et cetera, all united by this potent notion of poetry and Blackness. Brothers and sisters were singing and crying and testifying within days of meeting each other. People gathered like long-lost relatives. As if continuing a conversation they'd begun before they met. Which of course is always true with Black people. Is it more true with any other people on earth? Where does all that beauty come from? Where did Cave Canem come from? Where does Barack Obama come from?

After considering Bobby Kennedy's talk of a future Negro president, Baldwin scoffed at the notion of needing white people to sanction it. If one must ask permission to be free, it ain't freedom. He also scoffed at the notion that having a Negro president in forty years could suddenly fix the country's very fucked-up racial history. The irony, of course, is that Bobby Kennedy's prediction for America seemed, for a moment, true. It seemed, for a moment, we had come around a big bend on the racial mountain. We got President Barack Obama. But it's unlikely Bobby Kennedy considered the difference between a *Negro* president and a *Black* president. Or an African American president. Barack Obama seemed to have struggled with the distinctions himself. Me too, Brother. I have to say to a few Black people and a couple white people, *I am not your nigger*. But I've never really said to anyone *I am not your Negro*. The ending of *I Am Not Your Negro* implies Baldwin might have titled the film *I Am Not Your Nigger*. That's what he says near the end of the film. He never says, "I am not your Negro."

3.

Baldwin is not confused about where Black beauty comes from. It comes from Black people simply being themselves. End of discussion. But how did Black people get to be beautiful in the first place? What makes Black people Black people? Black ain't the same as Negro? Or African American? Several tribes from regions of Africa are captured, shackled, shipped, whipped, cropped, killed, submitted to every variety of violence—what does the violence do to them? Given all that has transpired and continues to transpire against Black people's existence, it would not be unreasonable to seek vengeance. Has any other group of people in the whole of history ever been more systematically, more publicly enslaved? We are the only group of humans to be constitutional property, to be owned like farm animals and equipment, like machines of commerce, industry in America. Superhuman and subhuman at the same time in America. House thief and housekeeper in America.

The work of convincing others you are human is a matter of power. Certainly power can be tangled into vengeance, violence. Did the history of violence in this country create Black people? Is our most potent notion of Blackness rooted in slavery, essentially? Would there be no Blackness without slavery? Would there be no whiteness without slavery? Baldwin writes, "A vast amount of the energy that goes into what we call the Negro problem is produced by the white man's profound desire not to be judged by those who are not white, not to be seen as he is, and at the same time a vast amount of the white anguish is rooted in the white man's equally profound need to be seen as he is." The white man has some work to do to convince other human beings he is human too. It is not unreasonable, whether or not he is a devil, a monster, if not a descendant of some devilish monster. What would you expect the enslaved, in their struggle to be as free as humanly possible, to do to their enslavers?

When they found themselves alone, these broken tribes of farmers, hunters, mothers, sons, and daughters (let us never call them slaves; let us call them the first Black people); when they found themselves with downtime together, what did they do? They weren't thinking about white people, for one thing. They found ways to communicate. They made themselves into instruments of music. Certainly there were Black people who made themselves into instruments of vengeance and instruments of fear and submission. But here I want to say art has always been Black people's response to violence. Art has always been Black people's response to beauty and to being alive. The impulse to make art is probably true for humanity in general, but that whole slavery thing makes the kind of art Black people make a *little bit different*. We are the kind of people who can turn Bible hymns into battle songs. *Yea, though I walk through the valley of the shadow of death, I will fear no evil*. Our response to violence has been gospel, jazz, hip-hop, Nina Simone, James Brown, Public Enemy; it has been Cave Canem. It has not always been a respectable response. Our response has every lifted voice singing "till *earth* and *heaven* ring," but it also has gutbucket voices singing for hell and high water. It's got white voices in it too. In the instrumental version of "The Star-Spangled Banner" Jimi Hendrix wields his guitar like a flamethrower; he makes it cry and screech like people crying and screeching amid fighter jets and sirens. It's a critique of Vietnam, but it's also a celebration of America's almost miraculous wildness; it celebrates destruction and self-destruction: a proper reflection of how this country thrives and ruins. My guess is this is exactly the way Francis Scott Key intended it to be played. He just had to wait for the electric guitar to be invented and for Jimi Hendrix. Maybe Key knew America's future would be that of a troubled family: infant tantrums, juvenile delinquency, and a mess of other violent growing pains. That's in Jimi's version of the song. Is this feeling in the song because Hendrix hears the American dream, or is it in the song because Hendrix is the dream? One Black man playing "The Star-Spangled Banner" that way should be evidence for what I'm suggesting here today: It is our song. It is our nation.

I know it doesn't seem that way. Key was not thinking of Black folks. Just the whole ironic nature of documents like the Declaration of Independence, the Bill of Rights, and the Constitution for Black folks could make a brother take a knee during the anthem. I read such gestures, if you know the Colin Kaepernick story, as a totally patriotic display of the brother's disappointment, even outrage, at the state of things. But it was not a disavowal of the song and the dream—which is really all about the kind of courage he displayed. Even if it was just a minor display.

Francis Scott Key could never have imagined slavery when he was talking about "the land of the free." He could not have truly imagined what freedom might mean in America's future. In fact, he is on record saying Africans in America were "a distinct and inferior race of people." He pushed for the Liberia Movement—essentially sending "free slaves" back to Africa. None of this makes the creed of the song any less significant. We've heard it enough times to get the gist of it: *the land of the free and the home of the brave.* It's in every stanza. It's a line of promise. It's a refrain. You hear this enough in grade school, and before sporting events, inaugurations, graduations, you might start believing it, you might start expecting it, you might want to make it come true. You might be a strange, lovely Black woman who encounters a strange and lovely Black man, each trying to write poems and trying to live free and brave, and you might actually be free and brave enough to invite several other strange, lovely Black people to be free and brave in poems about, among many things, themselves and their parents and brothers and sisters, the white people who are so afraid of them, the white people we are so afraid of.

So, yes, one Black man playing "The Star-Spangled Banner" is evidence that this is one nation. I'm on the side of Baldwin. I don't know how he felt about the Black national anthem. But I know he liked good music. "The Star-Spangled Banner" is our song. And not just because of Memorial Day, the Fourth of July. This is our song. This is our nation: we share it, we defend it. We are instruments of music. Admittedly, it's a very complicated music, because this is a very complicated nation. That's why we can hear it played by Hendrix with vengeance and then sung with something close to transcendence by Marvin Gaye at the NBA All-Star Game in 1983. The song is as complicated as the man who sings "Let's Get It **On**" as well as "What's Going **On**." America lives between those two songs. If you know "Sonny's Blues," by a young James Baldwin (about a Black man who is transformed when he hears his brother, a recovering heroin addict, play jazz) and if you know "Going to Meet the Man," by an older James Baldwin (about a white man who is transformed when he sees a Black man burned alive) then you know America also lives between those two stories. We need all the stories and all the stories between the stories, all the songs, all the poems.

4.

After singing "The Star-Spangled Banner" Marvin Gaye tells an interviewer sometimes you have to leave this country to love it. He'd been having a hard time here: divorce, taxes, depression. Not long after *Here, My Dear,* he found himself in self-exile in a small Belgian beach town in the off-season. He was trying to kick his drug habit. I've visited this place, Ostend, Belgium, twice. I'm not saying I'm the reason, but the first time, I walked all over town asking about him and there was nothing there; when I went back a few years later, they had a tour. But it just takes you to a bunch of unimpressive addresses. He could do nothing but get clean there. He sanctified himself. In the DVD I bought while I was there, he jogs, flirts, plays music and basketball. After a long while singing to himself and God and occasionally at the local casino, he returned to America. He was a man trying to be more free. One hears all this in his "Star-Spangled Banner" in 1983. He sings it like a song, not an anthem. Or it's just some other kind of very intimate anthem.

Something happened to him while he was exiled trying to rediscover or restore or revise himself. His voice isn't the same in any other songs. He was dead a year later, shot by his father.

I have seen what Black people can do with beauty. I have seen Black people make their complicated, contradictory, and fucked-up histories into poems. Little verbal engines. Wires of feeling. I'm not going to totally say it's artists that hear the dream of America best and then give this dream a shape, but I will say poets carry love in their defense, love in their loneliness and bewilderment, their doubt and genius. This is how we welcome Cave Canem in its twentieth year. I said Cave Canem was founded by teachers who had nothing in common beyond poetry and Blackness. I should have added, they had in common what they taught us. They taught us personal life need not be separated from public or political life. They taught us, they taught me, to write in my room alone, but to always turn my gaze to the window on our country as well as to the mirror of family and reflection, and to always leave a door into this room where you all are welcome to enter, eat, dance, and rest. We celebrate Black poets of complex Americanness. We must love this country better than it loves us. And this country must love us better than we love ourselves. I'm going to stop talking about it. I'm going to let you listen to Marvin Gaye sing it.

Afaa M. Weaver,
Born 1951

Dear Bear Poet,

 I read *A Fire in the Hills* four or five times & started four or
five different blurbs. Each time I had a different appreciation for this
book & your body of work. "Afaa Weaver is our poet of memory &
family." That was how my earliest blurb started. I think of you as one
of few male poets in the family of Gwendolyn Brooks. A love for the
local & social, a love for private as well as public Blackness. Your roots
in Black working class & Black arts aesthetics make you one of our
truest sons of Gwendolyn Brooks. The epigraph also nods to Hayden
& "Middle Passage": a big root in your poet tree. Your work has the

formal virtuosity I associate with Hayden. Along with the candor & interiority & toughness of Clifton.

This book's narrative vigor reminds me of the poems in *My Father's Geography*. The poems display intimacy & intensity across broad personal & cultural subjects. I first saw your poems in one of Ed Ochester's early Pitt anthologies. I believe I also first heard your name via a Pittsburgh playwright, the late great Rob Penny. So I've always associated you with Sonia Sanchez & maybe Lamont Steptoe & the black working class poets. I remember many poets spoke highly of you at the old annual black writers conference in Philadelphia. I don't know. I'm trying to say I am not surprised by the political directness of these poems.

These new poems keep watch, hold vigil in real time. They marry the "now" of racism & injustice with the history of racism & injustice. Titles like "Blues in Five/Four, the Violence in Chicago" & "Sirens of Saigon" reflect on the era of political urgency & upheavals half a century before. In "When I Think of Vietnam" you write: "This poem must resist all things that kill, things that add to war's breath." The sweep of these poems "resist all things that kill, things that add to war's breath."

You resist all categories "singing southern chants for spells" & "spinning top hairdos." Your syntax holds the movement of a train along the N line to Brooklyn: "passengers locked into the places of their own lives, working or not working." Those lines point to the care for working-class folks across your body of work.

This is a cohesive book born of political urgency & political memory. This is a book of resistance & freedom, of elegy & praise song. Political elegies blend into cultural elegies, cultural elegies blend into intimate elegies. Whimsical, spiritual & political intensities meld. "A Poem for Freddie Gray, Baltimore" is adjacent to "To Malcolm X On His Second Coming."

But ultimately, it's just nice to watch you continue making poems. I can only think of Brooks when I think of the humor throughout these poems. She shares your mix of formal & informal mischiefs, your mix of lyric vernacular. Your career has been Brooksian in work ethic, in virtuosity, & in its praise of the intimacies & solidarities of Blackness.

You are a North Star for us poets who know one is always only becoming a poet. I spent an afternoon listening to "Back Spin of Hope" with Joel/Renegade in Pittsburgh. I played the text through the computer's automated voice & we talked about the form. We should have recorded ourselves. We talked about that poem at length! We never decoded it exactly. Is that a form? Instead, we just marveled at your lyricism. Thanks for sharing the poems. Feel free to use anything here into the blurb:

Blurb for *A Fire in the Hills*

The splendid *A Fire in the Hills* holds lyrical inventories, telepathic persona poems, "southern chants for spells," "spinning top hairdos" & invented forms. Afaa Weaver can write any kind of poem you can imagine. He is our Black nonconforming formalist breaking free of form to shape a spirit of witness. He is both our sage bear poet of wisdom & our wily fox poet of mischief. He's been writing long enough to resist all classifications except that of Master Poet.

Tony Hoagland, Born 1953

Tony Hoagland died of pancreatic cancer at the age of sixty-four in Santa Fe, New Mexico. Because Hoagland was born in Fort Bragg, North Carolina, it is unclear whether he should be remembered as a southerner or product of the military ward. Fort Bragg is named for native North Carolinian Confederate General Braxton Bragg, who was generally considered the least victorious & least popular general of the Civil War. My younger brother was also born there. Our father was in the army. Hoagland's father was an army doctor, so Hoagland grew up on various military bases in Hawaii, Alabama, Ethiopia, & Texas. *What Narcissism Means to Me* is a fairly confessional title & subtitle for his best book, published in 2003. My favorite is *Donkey Gospel*. Religious hymns of a jackass, a dickhead, a wiseass, a poet filled with wit & fire, the belligerent sweet ruin of Frank O'Hara's nephew. Most of the battles in which Bragg engaged ended in defeat. In *Donkey Gospel*, Hoagland begins the poem "Adam and Eve": "I wanted to punch her right in the mouth and that's the truth," but critics seem less interested in his views of women. He had an older sister, & a twin brother who died of a drug overdose in high school. Once upon a time a white man took a Black family into the woods. In Andre Tarkovsky's *Stalker*, a writer & a teacher are led by a stalker into a place called "the zone," a bereft mysterious space that has spread from the sight of some kind of alien attack years before. In Alex Garland's 2018 film *Annihilation*, a psychologist, a physicist, a chemist, a geologist & a biologist head into the shimmer, a land that has spread from an alien meteor that strikes Texas at the start of the film. Once upon a time a white man took a Black family into the woods to a secret swimming hole. Once upon a time a white man removed his shirt & jumped into water & the Black children followed him in. "My message is it is impossible to pass on experience to others; we must live our own experience, we cannot inherit it," Andrei Tarkovsky told a room of aspiring filmmakers shortly before his death. They had time on their hands & the tools to create almost any desire. Once upon a time a white man took a Black family along a tangled woodsy dirt road to an inland lake full of white people whose eyes followed the two little Black children wading in the water. The surface of the lake trembled the way when, at weigh-in, Ali's body shamed the crowd, the camera trembled slightly. Do you feel apologies have no value in this climate? Are your children dumbstruck & afraid? The late-great Tony Hoagland rests in peace.

Lynda Hull,
Born 1954

Lynda Hull, like Walt Whitman, not to mention Dorothy Parker, William Carlos Williams, Allen Ginsberg, W. S. Merwin, Anne Waldman, Patti Smith & Amiri Baraka, was born on the mystifying planet of New Jersey. Hull's poems are as incendiary as the lighter fluid inside the sturdy, stainless steel Zippo lighter she stole from her father, a spout of spitfire, when she ran away from home at sixteen. "I remember this the way I'd remember a knife against my throat: that night, after the overdose, you told me to count, to calm myself," Hull writes in "Counting in Chinese," a poem derived, one assumes, from Hull's years high as the moon on the lam in Chinatown, married to a gambler from Shanghai. Taking up her pen & mostly laying down her syringe, Hull was divorced & remarried to a poet by 1984, living on fugitive wonder & figurative language, lines of Hopkins & Akhmatova, in Arkansas & later Indiana. Hull sometimes read her poems wearing dangling earrings & ankle-strapped high heels with her flapper's hairdo dyed the same color as her beret. In addition to lighter fluid, Hull's poems display the properties of rain just before it evaporates. Hull's poems hold salt water: "Tide of Voices" in *Ghost Money* (1986), "Shore Leave" in *Star Ledger* (1991), "Rivers into Seas" in *The Only World* (1995), published a year after her death in a car crash in Provincetown a few miles from the beach. When she wakes on the other side, Hull spends the hours she's not writing poetry mulling figures of wonder with holy wine while listening to fugitive jazz.

Sometimes Bird appears with his horn on the cover of *Ornithology*. Having retained her uncanny ability to channel varieties of sound, Hull scats to Bird like Ella Fitzgerald, wiping sweat from her brow. Sometimes ghosts come by. When she was alive, Hull memorized the entirety of *The Bridge*, a fifty-six-page multi-section poem about the Brooklyn Bridge written by Hart Crane, Hull's favorite poet, in 1923 when he was twenty-three & working as a copywriter in Cleveland, nine years before his suicide. Hart Crane comes by sometimes. Hull regales him with passages of *The Bridge* long into the eternal evening.

POET ★ AA ALL STAR ★

PATRICIA SMITH

Patricia Smith,
Born 1955

The first time a six- or seven-year-old Chicago-born Patricia Smith was given an eye exam, she turned the writing on the wall into a series of abecedarian blues poems. A smith is essentially one who hammers, bends & welds a variety of complex & tenacious elements into tools, weapons & instruments. Kinds of smiths include, but are not limited to, the swordsmith, the gold- & coppersmith, the gun- & locksmith. Kinds of Smith poems include, but are not limited to, the dramatic monologue, the political elegy, the sonnet, the ghazal, the golden shovel, the constant lovely love poem. A smith's desk is an anvil. Smith can make & repair complex chains of attachment & chains of syntax as well as the complex clasp on the gold chain worn by a young trash-talker walking on a basketball court in sunglasses, blue jeans & tube socks because he does not want to hoop in his new Air Jordans. A smith works in a smithy. Between *Life According to Motown* & *Incendiary Art*, Smith worked on *Teahouse of the Almighty* & *Blood Dazzler* while raising her granddaughter. Ogun, god of blacksmiths for Yoruba practitioners, climbed down to earth on a spiderweb & gave the secret of metal to Black people. Smith fashions poems with the mettle a Black woman needs to live. Smith is a common surname among 2.4 million mostly African American Americans. You are very likely some kin to a smith. You may feel like someone floating in a swimming pool animated by lightning, reading Smith. It may feel like someone has kissed your scalp to instigate time travel. The eye doctor first mistook six- or seven-year-old Patricia Smith's poetic eye chart recitation for witchcraft, bebop &/or glossolalia. "Each of the child's ocular sockets contains extrasensory sight receptors that make you feel the way a fortune teller feels looking into crystal when you look into them," read the doctor's diagnosis. He was very likely the first to witness the vision of Patricia Smith. He certainly was not the last.

Lucie Brock-Broido,
Born 1956

Sweet William, her immortal Maine Coon cat, claims all the cats left in Pittsburgh upon the take-off of Lucie Brock-Broido in the late Seventies, escaping smoke to smoke, were waiting when she returned to read poetry a rainy September evening in 2014. Sweet William communicates across time & space with all of Lucie Brock-Broido's cats. I am one of those cats. A few years before she became eternal poetry, I invited her to read for the first time in her career in her birthplace. The whole night I felt like I was apologizing & cursing the oversight of all the poets ever to purr in the city. The supernatural sunsets crowning the Appalachian foothills glittered on the rivers & all the cats of those foothills purred "ichor" instead of "blood" on the bridges of the city. Cats purred seeking the contents of her noctuary. Long live Jack Gilbert, Gerald Stern & Lucie Brock-Broido. Sweet William says the Maine Coon was incorrectly declared extinct about the time Lucie was born, but its origins are unknown. Cats purred seeking the contours of her language between their ears. Upon a recognition of her mortality, her cats devised strategies to keep her alive. Some took photos or wayward yard-long strands of her supernatural hair, some wrote memoirs about her care, some cats murmured on the bridges. I met her at one of those parties poets throw themselves when they are thrown together. "In the green rooms of the Abandonarium." In the green room of the garden party, in the green room of the robber baron's library. The Maine Coon is rumored to be the descendant of Marie Antoinette's orphaned cats & a colony of raccoons. Sometimes Sweet William says he is the bastard child of a Siberian ushanka & a Squirrel Hill shtreimel. When Lucie Brock-Broido read that rainy September evening four years before her passing, wisps of Vesuvian smoke stoked the overthrow of hair falling blonde upon her verbal okey-dokes, a wink & scope, smoke returning to smoke.

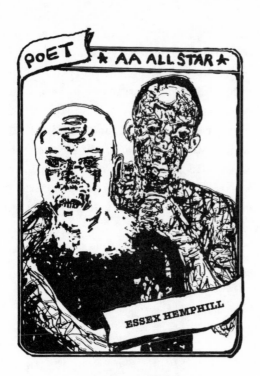

Essex Hemphill,
Born 1957

Essex Hemphill, born & raised in the age of infectious hungers, communicable longing, & the heartbreak of desire, died in 1995, having proclaimed in his poem "For My Protection," "We should be able to save each other." Hemphill proposed in the poem an official organization wherein a Black man could stroll Harlem, Wall Street, Hollywood, South Africa with his tongue untied without penalty of death, physical harm, or the snarls, stares, & snares of distraction & disaster. Hemphill's life was partly my life & possibly partly more or less yours. "Are you ready for whatever whenever?" Hemphill asks not only those sporting S-curls, dreadlocks, & styles that never expire, but the guardians of the endangered & admirers of the priceless. Born & raised & run around the districts of America, Hemphill proposed in the poem an organization to help Black men survive & alluded to a rich catalog of love without fear of Black men in black jackets & caskets of flowers, of the people who love them, & of dreamers on a train moving through a countryside of cattle grazing below a Confederate flag painted on a barn side. Protection from underlying, undermining fault lines & headlines. Protection from the hole of a blind bull's-eye, protection from the nurse's eyes & the doctors & angels gossiping at the bedside. Strike out without fear for love every day you are alive, suggests Hemphill's poem & existence. Strike out without fear & let your mouth fall open every day you are alive.

TWENTIETH CENTURY EXAMINATION

Part VI: What Happened to the Last of the Last Poets?

1971

Joni Mitchell releases *Blue*

Funkadelic releases *Maggot Brain*

Marvin Gaye releases *What's Going On*

1972

David Bowie releases *The Rise and Fall of Ziggy Stardust and the Spiders from Mars*

1973

Marvin Gaye releases *Let's Get It On*

Stevie Wonder releases *Innervisions*

1975

One Flew Over the Cuckoo's Nest the film

John Ashbery publishes *Self-Portrait in a Convex Mirror*

1976

US Bicentennial

1978

The Wiz

1979

Michael Jackson releases *Off the Wall*

Prince releases *Prince*

Octavia Butler publishes *Kindred*

Adrienne Rich
Musing on Modes of Gender?

Audre Lorde
Musing on Womanhood?

Octavia Butler
Musing on *Kindred*?

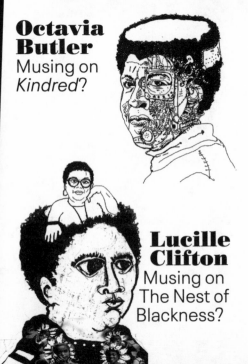

Lucille Clifton
Musing on The Nest of Blackness?

126. In 1963, when William Carlos Williams, Louis MacNeice, and Robert Frost met Sylvia Plath at the crossroads between heaven and hell, what was the joke she told them?

127. Is reading looking, is looking reading, is drawing writing as well?

128. What's the one thing you can never do?

129. Who would play Adrienne Rich and who would play Audre Lorde in a two-woman off-Broadway play about the pair?

130. Is it crazy to consider everything after 1968 contemporary?

131. Who remembers that *In the Heat of the Night* won the Oscar for Best Picture in 1968?

132. Do you think Oscar-winning movies, Grammy-winning songs, or prize-winning poems tell us anything about the era in which they were won?

133. Can you use *caesura* in an everyday sentence?

134. Do you agree one of Gwendolyn Brooks's best books was *In the Mecca*, her last with a major publisher?

135. Are you one of the people who think the Apollo moon landing was fake?

136. What is the relationship between a poet like Allen Ginsberg and the rise of the middle class in postwar America?

137. Is it still possible to build a career on a few decent poems?

138. When will someone make a movie about Elizabeth Bishop abroad?

139. Who says what's American?

140. Would the poem "Diving into the Wreck" be on your list of the most influential poems of the last century?

141. Did you know when Adrienne Rich won the National Book Award for *Diving into the Wreck* in 1974, she shared the stage and read a speech she cowrote with two other nominees, Alice Walker and Audre Lorde?

142. Did you know Rich shared the 1974 National Book Award prize with Allen Ginsberg's *The Fall of America: Poems of These States*?

143. When you brush your hair, do you use a mirror to see all the sides of yourself?

144. Do you sometimes confuse James Wright and Jay Wright, or James Wright and Franz Wright?

145. Wouldn't you like to know what people who have been born when autumn begins in Martins Ferry, Ohio, think when they read James Wright's poem "Autumn Begins in Martins Ferry, Ohio"?

146. What happened to Franz Wright?

147. Is it true that when Robert Lowell died in a cab in 1977, a manuscript about the Boston Brahmin was lost?

148. Didn't Frank Stanford come back from the dead?

149. Is Maya Angelou's poem "Still I Rise" the sort of poem that must be taught, or can a reader get it without guidance?

150. Do you recall whether or not there was a heat wave the first time you read *Thomas and Beulah*?

151. Is it possible to name any generation's key poets without omitting someone?

152. If Wallace Stevens can be of "three minds" and still be fairly narrow-minded, how many blackbirds do you suppose populate the trees of Gwendolyn Brooks's mind?

153. Who profits from John Berryman's madness?

154. Who saw *The Deer Hunter*, *The Wiz*, and *Midnight Express* at age seven at the drive-in?

155. Who else heard "Maggot Brain" in the womb?

156. Don't the Language poets and New York School poets claim John Ashbery belongs to them?

157. Do you think most of the world rotates between the poles of "What's Going On" and "Let's Get It On" by Marvin Gaye?

158. Is it better to be judged by your peers or by the general public?

End of Twentieth Century Examination, Part VI?

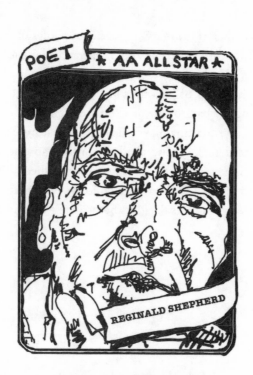

POET ★ AA ALL STAR ★

REGINALD SHEPHERD

Reginald Shepherd,
Born 1963

The shepherd in Reginald Shepherd is derived from the job first assigned to a village boy who spent his days hunting the sheep he heard babbling in the woods & spent his nights giving names to the stars. Shepherd of *Otherhood*. Shepherd of the lantern fire, shepherd of the antique lyre of *Orpheus in the Bronx*. By the time he was a young man, babblers gathered around the shepherd saying words he heard as poems. If he let the sheep indoors, they broke the quiet. A wolf might rise or rain might fall if the sheep were left outside. Shepherd of Pensacola, Florida, from the Bronx, shepherd of cancer, shepherd of brushes with death moving over the flock, shepherd of *Some Are Drowning*. Shepherd of *Red Clay Weather*. *Fata Morgana* was King Arthur's sister, a maker of trouble & mirage over bodies of frailty & water. Shepherd of *Fata Morgana*. The *Angel, Interrupted* must be durable in a downfall. The shepherd in Reginald Shepherd is derived from a job looking after the songs of creatures like the serpent curled in syntax, the ballad riding the back of the blackbird, the Hart Crane, the Adorno echo of the sheep squatting like clouds in the pasture. The look of the sheep & shepherd, feeling how small all our lives appear when viewed from the stars, is never sweeter than the milk the sheep offer the shepherd, who then offers it to the village children, who in turn share their portions with village adults & elders before the milk can spoil.

David Cloud Berman,
Born 1967

If you have ever read "Now II" from *Actual Air*, the only book of poems published by the late David Berman, & wondered why there is
no "Now I," you will find the answer in Denis Johnson's book of poems *The Incognito Lounge*, where the model poem "Now" resides. The
poems & poets share vipers & refrains of vapor. Berman sang poorly
but poetically before crowds confounded by the name of his band. "Is
the problem that we can't see, or is it that the problem is beautiful to
me?" Berman used to sing. David Cloud Berman was born David Craig
Berman but changed his middle name after the death of his friend
Dave Cloud in 2015. Berman is the poet one imagines as Apollinaire

if Apollinaire's mother was an Ohio schoolteacher & his father sweet-talked politicians to death. David Berman, according to David Berman, acquired Denis Johnson's mailing address & sent Johnson *Actual Air*, possibly with the page of "Now II" turned down. (The bend in the horizon obstructed by mountains disrupting the end of the line.) Though Denis Johnson did not make the "Now" connection when *Actual Air* arrived, he told me he recalled his strange & pleasant feeling reading the book. "I'm afraid I've got more in common with who I was than who I am becoming," Berman used to sing.

A Frank Stanford Lyric Speech Act Test with Visions

"I dreamed the night was a horse / With its eyes shut"

Lyric Speech Acts

This lyric speech act essay prompt offers an engagement with *The Battlefield Where the Moon Says I Love You*, the five-hundred-page, mid-twentieth-century epic by the legendary, visionary orphan poet-saint Frank Stanford. *The Battlefield* records the visions of Francis, a twelve-year-old protagonist who is an apprentice outlaw bluesman, a vernacular alchemist, and a wandering witness. This lyric speech act maps how a writer (Stanford, you, the test maker) navigates the battlefield. Your work here requires contemplations of 1) personal character development, 2) the impact of setting on your body, and 3) the craft and mobility of your survival (your anti-suicidal) poetics. While it is possible to leave yourself psychically, ideally you want to leave yourself somewhere between five to ten years of experience in the battlefield before undertaking this act. You must erase the lines between thesis, antithesis, and synthesis while establishing boundaries. Employ abundant specific, detailed examples, including dates and names, from your own personal library of dreams. It's OK to revise the details—the test maker is not allowed to grade you on the truth of your dreams. When dealing with the visions you may not always have a clear understanding of the meaning, and therefore you don't necessarily have to understand.

PART I. Lyric Speech Act Essay Subtest Study Graphic

Bio of Birth: Blossoming Moon, Blossoming Whole Notes, Blossoming Black Holes

Fill in the cluster of holes versus moons to chart the sonic lines of birth and battle. The poet tows a hammer up a tree. He makes a hammock of the lake. What other resonances emanate where the moon is a whole note? *The Battlefield Where the Moon Says I Love You* foretells the events of Frank Stanford's brief yet eternal life. *The Battlefield Where the* smells coming over evening say I love you? Were we born in love with death, or do we grow in love with life? *The Battlefield Where the* wind makes mystery sound like misery coming over the water. *The Battlefield Where the* wind makes mystery look like misery coming over the lake. *The Battlefield Where the Poet* sleeps with a loaded gun in the Bible drawer. *The Battlefield Where the Poet* sleeps like a loaded gun in the Bible drawer like a dog with a cruel master, like a dog who follows a boy to war.

When you have completed the chart of holes, moons, or whole notes, compose a speech act. Make a discursive, lyric language figuring the multiple visions of Frank Stanford on the battlefield.

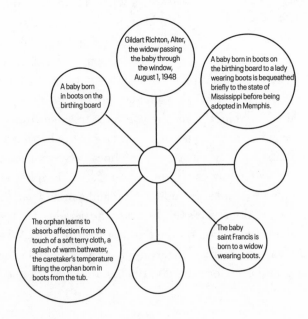

PART II. Lyric Speech Act Essay

The 1977 original cover depicts a nightmare scene of death and grief from the Vietnam War. A figure of incarnate grief crouches over bodies half-covered by a tarp; to the left an ominous official pant leg can be seen departing the scene. The public-domain image is an especially strange cover, especially when compared to the 2000 cover. It depicts a surreal pastoral vernacular. A young, solemn-looking Black man stares behind a mysterious floating orb, a moon, a crystal ball.

In preparation of the lyric speech act, write a lengthy journal entry from the point of view of St. Francis, the Freak Count Hugo, Sonny Liston, Elvis Presley, or Henri Rousseau on the battlefield. Are we born in love with life, or do we grow in love with death? Where is the battlefield? The feet below the groves and clover meadows do no marching. The path below the light flooding the flowers. Each of the 15,283 lines on the map bleeds the red of melancholy and mischief; the red of the devil's tongue. St. Francis and the Neglected Wife, St. Francis and the falling water, St. Francis and the Black Angel. Francis versus the greed of sap sucker mosquitoes. The temple is made with majestic fists. There are visions that cannot be seen by the blind.

The essay should be completed over a single evening under moonlight and the supervision of the test maker, a shadowy figure. . . . Before the witch doctor teacher can tell you the last known tale of the last orphan saint Francis, the shotgun schoolhouse groans like a freight train of bluesmen at a crossroads. Your teacher sighs, it's Frank's ghost, a dark horse nuzzling his side.

the battlefield
where the moon says I
love you

a poem by
frank stanford

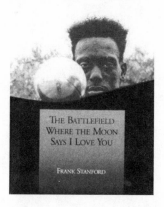

PART III. Lyric Speech Act Essay Subtest Study Graphic

Goggles of Frankness

An engagement with the overlapping idiomatic as well as symphonic dualities between Frank, the metaphysical bluesman, and Francis, the alchemical saint, should prompt a comparable multidimensional duality and, if you will, frankness, in the test taker. Complete the Venn diagram of Frank and Francis. The battlefield spheres are made of loopholes and manholes, wormholes and rabbit holes, eyeholes, pie holes, and inverted circles. In each battlefield sphere, fill in the contrasts between poet and persona. Where the spheres blur, write in their similarities. Then, over seven to ten days, compose a lyric speech act wherein you shape the war you wage with yourself. Does your life vanish between objects and subjects? If death represents the only failure, there can be no failure as long as you are alive. Your lyric speech act should dwell with its frankness on the line. Successful acts will reveal the absence of lines.

Frank   Francis

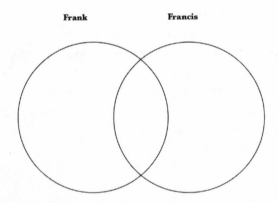

PART IV. Lyric Speech Act Essay

When anyone asked him if he was half-Black, the orphan said, "There was Blackness on all sides of the infantry." Armed confusions between natures are old as lost time. The battlefield holds the ephemeral and transitory nature of ghosts, hands, and singing knives. It may be that regions of the orphan poet's expressions resembled the green foamy nature of Jean Toomer coming and going like the humid sundowns around Subiaco Academy, the Ouachita Mountains. The areas of the mind enthroned and unknown are evidence of spiritual electricity. The troubadour ticker tape ticket taker dreamed a starlight bleeding onto barbed wire like hot milk, dreamed a father unstringing his son from the tree of knowledge, dreamed his twin a few short years in the future coughing up clover underground. When forced to choose between the nature of the body, which keeps you rooted in the field, and the nature of the mind, which keeps you rooted in the sky, the stars and supernatural moonlight, which nature should you arm? Why did Frank Stanford die?

PART V. Contemplate the Following Perspectives

Perspective 1

The orphan poet-saint Francis versus Mountain Home. The orphan poet-saint Francis wins versus the two hundred fireside poets looking down from the mountain. The orphan poet-saint Francis versus the underground aviary of angels cast from Hell. The orphan poet-saint Francis wins versus the floodwater because he dreams a levee. The orphan poet-saint Francis versus the community cemetery, the orphan poet-saint Francis reverses the terrible loneliness of the cemetery, the orphan poet-saint Francis converses with his shadow of ghosts, a sky of tree leaves copper as comets. The dark inclinations of the orphan poet-saint Francis along with access to the realms and waters of Blackness contributed greatly to the battles.

Perspective 2

He dreamed up a typewriter big as a combustion baby tractor under the weeping willow tree called black stallion and typed one five-hundred-page-long sentence in a night. He dreamed a one-word paragraph for the spruce on the battlefield, a lullaby for the Sugar Pines; he dreamed a musical for the brown-barked *Libocedrus*, the king of conifers of the earth, and an epic for the tree most like a starved weeping warhorse looking for its rider.

Perspective 3

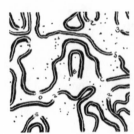

He leaned into the typewriter like a mad farmer tilling for gold at midnight, like a mad jockey racing his shadow in moonlight, like the mad farmer's widow riding the tractor for her children, like the mad jockey's bride shooing the horse's shadow from the church window. Every creative is a message from the heavens. Every feeling is a message from the earth's gravity. Every beautiful thought is proof God's most tangible kingdom is in your head. The feet below the groves and clover meadows do no marching. The path below the light flooding the flowers. There is no trace of the orphan catching up with his ghosts late in life or death.

Essay Task

Make a discursive, lyric language figuring the multiple visions of Frank Stanford on the battlefield. State and develop your own music.

Folk Stone

(previously titled "Frank Stanford as a Child of Alphabet City")

In my next life   let me be   dear black bird
Born with a foot   on the ass   of all assholes

None of them will remember me
More startled than starlight or starling last year   hidden

In the bushes   beside a river   running down the valley
In my next life   let me be   dear black bear

Strong enough to pull my childish true enemy
From the dark village   down the street

Where Monk's imitators play   the same nonlinear blues
I spend the lonely evenings playing

Force him to comb the underworld   for the book
I left beside a girl   on a subway

Covered in footnotes   & illegible handwriting
Dream versus sincerity   Thinking versus feeling

Machine versus engine   Shade versus shadow
The people who come after you   versus the people behind you

Anything versus everything   Poem versus Piano
If I live to be a four-year-old   Black girl   again

My sky-black dress   will never be as black   as my afro
If I live to be a ten-year-old   shotgun   again

Black as an anvil   full of buckshot   raise me   with my mother
In the most   southern & southernmost   of the Carolinas

Force our enemies to gather   all the stones   in a beautiful meadow
While singing   strange godly gospels   to pass the time

TWENTIETH CENTURY EXAMINATION

Part VII: Where Do Poets Come From?

1980
Launch of Cable News Network (CNN)

1981
Launch of MTV

1982
Alice Walker publishes *The Color Purple*

1984
Mary Oliver wins the Pulitzer Prize for Poetry for *American Primitive*

1985
Michael Jackson and Lionel Richie, USA for Africa release "We Are the World"

1986
The space shuttle *Challenger* explosion

1987
Toni Morrison publishes *Beloved*

Rita Dove wins the Pulitzer Prize for Poetry for *Thomas and Beulah*

1988
The Dark Room Collective founded

1989
Tiananmen Square protests

Fall of the Berlin Wall

Alice Walker
Musing on Her Generation?

Nate Mackey
Musing on Irritable Mystic?

Sharon Olds
Musing on Lines of Existence?

Rita Dove
Musing on *Thomas and Beulah*?

Harryette Mullen
Musing on "Muse & Drudge"?

Gwendolyn Brooks
Musing on Her Visions?

159. Do you know what I mean when I say the Black Mountain poets are to the Abstract Expressionist movement as the Black Arts poets are to the Black Power movement?

160. Where do you find the influence of W. S. Merwin these days?

161. Is "make it new" essentially the enduring motto of America?

162. Isn't whatever comes next in this passionately schizophrenic country bound to surprise us?

163. Who remembers when the guy falls from the bridge in *Saturday Night Fever*?

164. Are all muses full of negative capability?

165. Who remembers Mary Oliver won a Pulitzer Prize for Poetry for *American Primitive* in 1984?

166. Is *American Primitive* a suitable title for a Mary Oliver biopic?

167. Did Alex Haley's *Roots* influence Alice Walker's *The Color Purple* or Toni Morrison's *Beloved*?

168. Can you believe racists imprisoned Nelson Mandela for twenty-seven years?

169. In the sentence "*Beloved* author Toni Morrison has died," aren't there two shadows cast by *beloved*?

170. What's to be done if technology has more influence on cultural movements than writers and artists?

171. Who is the new Clayton Eshleman?

172. Would there be room for Charles Bukowski in your poetry family?

173. Who can account for the present given so such unaccounted history?

174. Who stopped watching *Jeopardy!* after Alex Trebek shaved his mustache?

175. What will happen to the poetry of Muriel Rukeyser, Pat Parker, May Swenson, and Diane Wakoski if we don't fit them into our poetic genealogy?

176. Who am I forgetting?

177. Does the muse of fame or the muse of glory have more sway over history?

178. Why can't your muse invent your story?

179. Did I tell you I met a writer who meant to have "whatever what is is is what I want" from Galway Kinnell's "Prayer" tattooed on his arm, but it's misquoted as "whatever is is is what I am"?

180. What did you love in Carolyn Forché's *The Country Between Us*, and why have you forgotten it?

181. Didn't Allen Grossman say the subject of poetry is always poetry?

182. Late in the visionary series covering decades of near-random poetry and events, what if the audience discovers it's all the dream of a Black middle-aged present-day high school AP English teacher?

183. Do you enjoy Mary Oliver's poems, but find that you've never discussed her in an academic setting?

184. Is it foolish to ask which poems written in any era impact public opinion?

185. Is it possible to grasp a word's etymology, connotations, semantic relationships, and practical usage, and still not grasp its poetry?

186. If you don't see suffering's potential as art, will it remain suffering?

End of Twentieth Century Examination, Part VII?

Introduction to *Wicked Enchantment: Selected Poems*

What we have here is a sterling, one-of-a-kind record of what it meant to be the late great poet Wanda Coleman. I will offer a few introductory comments, but let it be said: in life and in poetry, Wanda Coleman always preferred to speak for herself.

In Wanda's introduction to her chapbook *Greatest Hits 1966–2003*, published by Pudding House Press in 2004, she wrote:

> Eager to make my mark on the literary landscape, I got busy finding the mentors who would teach me in lieu of the college education I could not afford. As a result, I have developed a style composed of styles, sometimes waxing traditional, harking to the neoformalists, but most of my poems are written in a sometimes frenetic, sometimes lyrical free verse, dotted with literary, musical, and cinematic allusions, accented with smatterings of German, Latin, Spanish, and Yiddish, and neologisms, and rife with various cants and jargons, as they capture my interest, from the corporate roundtables to the streets.

First of all, the syntax of that second sentence is breathtaking. Second of all, what could I say to follow that? Maybe something about my own true introduction to her?

In the summer of 2001, I shared the stage with Wanda at the Schomburg Center for Research in Black Culture's 75th Anniversary Africana Heritage Festival. The reading, "A Nation of Poets: Wordsmiths for a

New Millennium," included Coleman and myself along with Amiri Baraka, Staceyann Chin, Sonia Sanchez, and Patricia Smith. It's not a very detailed memory. I was too awed to truly pay attention to anybody's poems (my own included). I mostly only remember the "frenetic, sometimes lyrical" (*neologismic? languafied?*) sound of Wanda's voice, her towering hair and bangles, her patterned fabrics and big glasses and big wicked laugh. I don't remember what she read, though I know she was writing some of her best work at the time and finally receiving some long-overdue attention. *Mercurochrome*, the book she published that year, would be a finalist for the 2001 National Book Award in Poetry, and 1998's *Bathwater Wine* had received the Lenore Marshall Prize from the American Academy of Poets. But Wanda was still announcing her presence and suspicions.

Upon our first real conversation, on a panel at an LA book festival the next year, Wanda "tore me a new one," as they say. She was a grenade of brilliance, boasts, and braggadocio. She burned and shredded all my platitudes about whatever poetry topic was at hand. She only softened when she understood/believed I was a fan. Recently, one of my mentors, a Black female poet of Wanda's generation, flatly said, "She was mean." She *could* be mean. It was a sharpness she honed over her years outside the care of poetry collectives, coalitions, and institutions. Her poems often record the mood of one who feels exiled, discounted, neglected. Imagine how mean the famously mean Miles Davis might have been had no one taken his horn playing seriously, and you will have a sense of Wanda's rage. I think some of it was misplaced. She had legions of fans. The actress Amber Tamblyn is a supreme Wanda disciple. Her other fans include Yona Harvey, Douglas Kearney, Dorothea Lasky, Tim Seibles, Annie Finch, experimentalists, formalists, feminists, spoken-word artists. She once told me the musician Beck is a big fan. There is no poet, Black or otherwise, writing with as much wicked candor and passion.

I have taught her poetry to my students for nearly all of my career. One of my oldest homemade writing exercises asks poets to devise their own American Sonnet after looking at Wanda's American Sonnets. Eventually I tried the exercise myself. I sent my first attempt, a poem titled "American Sonnet for Wanda C." (from *How to Be Drawn*, 2015), to Wanda a year or so before her death in 2013. I was imitating Wanda for years before meeting her. "The Things-No-One-Knows Blues" in *Hip Logic*, my second collection, is a direct nod to her poem "Things No One Knows" in *Bathwater Wine*. Yes, she let her guard down when she saw I was a fan. We became friends. I would never say close friends. But we were close poets. Our letters and exchanges concerned nothing but poetry. When Black Sparrow Press closed, I put Wanda in touch with Ed Ochester at the University of Pittsburgh Press. Ochester, who was my teacher at the University of Pittsburgh MFA poetry program, was editor for poets such as Sharon Olds, Etheridge Knight, and Larry Levis. Coleman wrote two terrific books for Pitt Press: *Ostinato Vamps* and *The World Falls Away*. Her passion for poetry made her sharp, warm, honest. Naturally, I loved her.

Wanda Coleman was a great poet, a real in-the-flesh, flesh-eating poet, who also happened to be a real Black woman. Amid a life of single motherhood, multiple marriages, and multiple jobs that included waitress, medical file clerk, and screenwriter, she made poems. She denounced boredom, cowardice, the status quo. Few poets of any stripe write with as much forthrightness about poverty, about literary ambition, about depression, about our violent, fragile passions. Wanda's poems speak for themselves.

In the margin of my secondhand copy of *Mad Dog Black Lady*, her first full-length collection, published by Black Sparrow Press in 1979, someone wrote, "Her world is a shriek." The poems do shriek sometimes. I open this new edition of Wanda's selected poems with "Wanda in Worry Land," where the refrains "I get scared sometimes" and "I have gone after people" echo the paradoxical vigor at the heart of her poems. They take the forms of aptitude tests, fairy tales, dream journals, and comic book panels. They combine manifesto and confession, inner and outer indictment, violence and tenderness, satire and sincerity. Her imitations of everyone from Lewis Carroll to Elizabeth Bishop to Sun Ra slip between homage and provocation. Themes and passions recur across the books in series like "Essay on Language," "Notes of a Cultural Terrorist," "Letter to My Older Sister," and especially in the American Sonnets series, which debuted in *African Sleeping Sickness* in 1990. Commenting on the series in the Adrienne Rich–edited *Best American Poetry 1996*, Wanda wrote:

> In this series of poems I assume my role as fusionist, delight in challenging myself with artful language play. I mock, meditate, imitate, and transform. . . . Ever beneath the off-rhyme, the jokey alliterations, and allusions, lurks the hurt-inspired rage of a soul mining her emotional Ituri.

All of that. Every poem is an introduction to Wanda Coleman. I keep her poems close because they never cease surprising me. In "Looking for It: An Interview," she says, "I want *freedom* when I write, I want the freedom to use any kind of language—whatever I feel is appropriate to get the point across." She never ceases revealing paths to get free.

Cornelius Eady Reading Introduction, 2003

If we were entering the long halls of Cornelius Eady's poems, I'd first direct your attention to the plaques detailing his awards: his fellowships from the Guggenheim Foundation, the Rockefeller Foundation, and the Lila Wallace Reader's Digest Fund; his nominations for the National Book Award and Pulitzer. While you perused his accolades, I'd begin to smile like a man who's proud of his job. You know, I know Mr. Eady, I'd boast. And though I wouldn't have time to share all of my Cornelius Eady anecdotes, I'd explain his importance as a cofounder of Cave Canem, with Toi Derricotte. How the two of them have literally changed the landscape of American poetry. And in your excitement you'd probably forget all that and then remember it again when you heard someone mention Cave Canem and the Harlem Renaissance together years from now.

We'd proceed along a wing under a banner reading "Autobiography and Imagination: Toward a Theory of Transformation in the Poetry of

Cornelius Eady." A few in our party would scratch their heads, and I'd say, Don't fret. Just think about how the personas in Eady's poems are often both mythological (e.g., the central figures in 2001's *Brutal Imagination*) and grounded in personal experience (e.g., the poems of 1997's *The Autobiography of a Jukebox* and 1995's *You Don't Miss Your Water*). He's able to turn his gaze outward to this country's cultural landscape as well as inward to the landscape of family and identity.

Then we'd reach the gallery for *Victims of the Latest Dance Craze*, and I'd say, Look at how Walt Whitman waltzes in the backdrop of Eady's work. Look at all the people in motion in these poems. Like Whitman he celebrates our collective history. And when necessary, like Whitman he condemns it. He remains one of the few American poets willing to confront race again and again in all of its complexity. Pointing to Eady's poem "Gratitude" in the gallery for *The Gathering of My Name*, I'd say, Look here where he says "I am a black American poet and my greatest weakness is an inability to sustain rage." And I'd add, pointing to the poem "Why Do So Few Blacks Study Creative Writing": Look here at his greatest strength, his ability to sustain tenderness. It's everywhere, I'd say: rage and tenderness struggling in the same breath.

We'd walk to another wing under a banner reading "A Poet According to His Blues," where we'd find Eady's blues poems displayed alongside the blues poems of Langston Hughes. Let me remind you that the blues are complicated: they are not only vehicles of pleasure, but of protest, I'd say as a few in our party began a bit of casual foot-tapping to the blues guitar piping into the room. Eady and Hughes share a love for the lucid diction and playfulness associated with the blues, I'd say. But there is also a current of sensual desire and intensity running through Eady's poems. A dimension of the blues I'm not sure we find in Hughes.

In the wing marked "From Page to Stage," we'd watch theatrical productions of *You Don't Miss Your Water*, the jazz opera *Running Man*, which was a 1999 Pulitzer finalist, and *Brutal Imagination* (starring Joe Morton, of *Terminator 2* fame). Eady's collaborator on all three projects, the avant-garde jazz composer Deidre Murray, would be on hand to discuss her understanding of performance and poetry in Eady's work. Joe would sign a few autographs.

Then we'd move on to the intimate, dimly lit gallery of *You Don't Miss Your Water*. And as we read the elegiac prose poems about the death of Eady's father, a few people would begin to weep. We'd all sigh and nod. And I'd get the feeling no one needed or wanted me to explain what was going on anymore and I'd stop talking. We'd continue on that way for a little while until we reached an auditorium where the poet himself would sit awaiting us, and I'd take a deep breath and say, "Excuse me, Mr. Eady, there are a few people here who'd like to meet you. I wonder if you might take a few moments to sing to us?"

Toi Tribute, 2012

The palms of my mother's hands are precious wild grass to me.
I wish to dance the dance of wild grass to the utmost of my heart.

—Kazuo Ohno

Sometimes the most unlikely activities call a great teacher to mind. It was during a recent three-hour kundalini yoga session, for example, that I thought of Toi. I don't do yoga normally—or to be honest, at all—but Yona persuaded me to join her for a session one evening. We found spots among a circle of fifteen or twenty wired/weird participants. Mats were spread out like little runways, or maybe magic carpets. I folded my blanket lengthwise and plopped down to the immediate tsking of a svelte elderly woman: "You must also remove your socks; there are chakras on the bottom of your feet!" *Chakras* sounded like something one should keep covered, but I obliged. I knew (and still know) next to nothing about yoga, but increasingly there was a feeling of familiarity. For one thing, the circle was very much like the opening and closing circles of Cave Canem. The people in the room were as serene and eager as the Cave Canem poets waiting to be led into a safe haven of poetry and fellowship by Toi and her Cave Canem cofounder, Cornelius Eady. It is Toi who, at various moments during these gatherings, is likely to offer a song. I recall a few modest bars of something by Billie Holiday, maybe Nina Simone's "Feeling Good," or, as often as not, some made-up tune. "Beautiful faces, beautiful faces," I have heard her sing to an audience of poets. I have heard her sing before students, friends, and colleagues over the years.

Toi Derricotte was the first poet, hers was the first poetry reading, I encountered outside the confines of college. My senior year in South Carolina I traveled to hear her read at a small liberal arts college an hour or so away from my even smaller liberal arts college. She did not sing that afternoon, but her warmth and candor made everyone lean forward. It is tempting to say her personality alone wowed me, but I think it was that her poetry eschewed artifice and persona in the name of clarity and presence. It had not occurred to me, reading Keats or Eliot or Hughes in my textbooks, that a poem could be such a faithful and fluid extension of the poet. When the reading was done I waited until the crowd thinned to introduce myself. She addressed me as if we were already close friends. I suspect many know this intimacy in her work and company. I knew by the end of that afternoon that I wanted to be her student. I remain her student.

Something about the kundalini teacher was familiar. She was a light-brown middle-aged woman who directed our movements, let fly a bit of new age–inflected encouragement, and managed the mellow music on her CD player while doing the poses herself. She seemed to drop into a zone of meditation, then emerge to make sure we were with her. It is no easy thing to be both leader and participant. Once during my first graduate class Toi turned out the lights and had us sit for a few moments in the darkness. There may have been candles. Before the lights went out, I caught the eye of a fellow grad student, one of my running buddies, a narrative poet whose poems featured dive jobs and truck drivers—it was a sort of slight, mutual eye roll we gave one another. I don't know what happened to him in the darkness, but I sat, perhaps with my head on the desk, waiting for instructions. It is possible Toi was also waiting for something, waiting to learn something. That was an early lesson she taught me: a teacher should be as open as her pupils. It is akin to a dance teacher who dances among her students. This sense of exchange is implicit in the mission of Cave Canem: a "safe haven" means safety not only for the students but for the teachers. In Toi's workshops the conversation above the poem was fluid and intimate. The poem itself was like something written on water: a site for discovery and transformation. I am thinking of her teaching style, but I am thinking as well of her poetry.

When I read Toi's latest book, *The Undertaker's Daughter*, I was reminded of the late butoh dancer Kazuo Ohno, who said our ability to move through pain reflects our ability to radically transform ourselves. Ohno is (I've been thinking about this too long maybe) an avatar of the undertaker and daughter in Toi's title. Check his Wikipedia entry and you'll find a slim, shirtless Asian man in a painted white face and black Mary Jane shoes. His dance style is a limber androgyny; gestures that marry improvisation and calculation, confidence and vulnerability. The guiding spirit of his work comes extraordinarily close to the spirit of Toi's work. Her poetry and her teaching fuse wisdom and curiosity, serenity and intensity. Consider the end of the title poem, "The Undertaker's Daughter," wherein the father is depicted variously as god, woman, and animal:

Once, when I opened the door & saw

him shaving, naked, the sole of his foot
resting on the toilet, I thought

those things hanging down were
udders. From then on I understood there was a

female part he hid—something
soft & unprotected

I shouldn't see.

Her poems insist on the power of intimacy and, perhaps more significantly, the power of vulnerability. To choose such a stance where most would choose the armor of bravado or detachment requires considerable will and skill. It also requires a capacity for "Negative Capability," a term Keats used in an 1817 letter: "That is when man is capable of being in uncertainties, Mysteries, doubts, without any irritable reaching after fact & reason." Viewed this way, Toi's poetry can be seen as more than a mere exercise in poetics.

I'd assumed before the kundalini session that yoga was all about fitness: a vaguely multicultural aerobics featuring young women in spandex. But I came to learn that the rigorous poses are meant to unlock the breath. Or rather, I remembered what Toi had already taught me: craft, or form, is a means to unlock feeling.

We were in something called a "cat pose." I was on my hands and knees with my nose a few awkward inches from the floor. When the instructor explained the philosophy of the bow, Toi came to mind. "The bow is sacred because it places the heart above the head," our instructor said. A bow makes the heart governor of the guarded mind.

There are various forms of bowing in Toi's poems. In "Invisible Dreams" the speaker seems to bow "like a / dog pawing a blanket / on the floor." In "Clitoris" a woman bows over her sex, lifting "the purplish hood back / from the pale white berry." In "Black Boys Play the Classics" boys bow over their instruments: "One white boy, three, sits / cross-legged in front of his / idols—in ecstasy." In "Grace Paley Reading," Paley bends (her heart above her regal head) as if in a bow:

Finally, the audience gets
restless, & they send me
to hunt for Grace. I find her
backing out of the bathroom, bending
over, wiping up her footprints
as she goes with a little
sheet of toilet paper, explaining,
"In some places, after the lady mops,
the bosses come to check on her.

I just don't want them to think
she didn't do her job."

It's easy to believe we'd send Toi "to hunt for Grace." The hunt has
been there since her earliest books. "Boy at the Paterson Falls" from
Captivity comes to mind: "I am thinking of that boy who bragged about
the day he threw / a dog over and watched it struggle to stay upright
all / the way down." The poem displays empathy for both the dog's
"rotting carcass on the rocks" and the child whose violence "must have
answered some need." Empathy is surely an element of grace—in Toi's
work, empathy is a necessary dimension of grace. She brings grace to
us as food. I could just about conclude this tribute with that truth.
Her teaching is rooted in grace; her openness is rooted in grace; her
fortitude is rooted in grace: aesthetic grace, intellectual grace, emotional grace.

Is grace something we can learn from her? I, for one, am still trying
to learn it. It requires steady work; it will always involve a bit of dis-
comfort. It is worthwhile. True and wondrous things happen when the
heart is above the head. The svelte woman beside me in the kundalini
yoga class claimed she could barely touch her toes when she began.
Now she is practically a human bow; with each breath she grows more
limber and lovely.

TWENTIETH CENTURY EXAMINATION

Part VIII: How Many of Your Muses Rest in Peace?

1990–1991

The Gulf War

1990

Nelson Mandela is released from prison after twenty-seven years

1992

April–May: Los Angeles riots over the Rodney King verdict

1993

Toni Morrison wins the Nobel Prize in Literature

1994

Yusef Komunyakaa wins the Pulitzer Prize for Poetry for *Neon Vernacular*

1995

O. J. Simpson trial

1996

Cave Canem, retreat for African American poets, is founded

Death of Tupac Shakur

1997

Death of Biggie Smalls

Radiohead releases *OK Computer*

2000

Lucille Clifton wins the National Book Award for Poetry for her volume *Blessing the Boats*

Gwendolyn Brooks dies

The American Muse of Destruction in the First of Two Gulf Wars

Brigit Pegeen Kelly
Musing on *Song*?

David Berman
Musing on *Actual Air*?

Tony Hoagland
Musing on What Narcissism Means to Him?

Toi Derricotte and Cornelius Eady
Musing on a Home for Black Poetry

Lynda Hull
Musing on *Star Ledger*?

Star Ledger

Lucille Clifton
Musing on the Age?

The Widening Spell of the Leaves

Larry Levis
Musing on *The Widening Spell of the Leaves*?

187. Did I ever tell you how encountering Gwendolyn Brooks's poem "The Mother" one lonely afternoon in college brought on tears that moved me to the path of a poet?

188. Don't we all hope a poem that prompts tears can withstand the sobering, scrutinizing gaze of time?

189. You're not one of those people who confuse Gwendolyn Brooks and Gwendolyn Bennett, are you?

190. Can you name any women poets of the Harlem Renaissance?

191. You're not one of those people who confuse Jack Gilbert and Jack Spicer, are you?

192. Did you know Denzel Washington played Melvin B. Tolson in a movie?

193. Where does Melvin B. Tolson go in your timeline of American poetry?

194. What do you know about Robert Creeley after he left Black Mountain?

195. Is it better to be a great poet or make a great poem?

196. When was the last time you read a poem by James Dickey, James Merrill, or James Schuyler?

197. Are you content contemplating the poets starring in a story of American poetry?

198. Does all history end and begin with your muses?

199. Do questions or answers create history?

200. Who is your muse of the Reagan era?

201. Are more of your muses in music or movies?

202. What should we say about Maya Angelou's poetry?

203. Where does Sterling Brown go?

204. Do you confuse Yeats with Auden, or Yeats with Keats?

205. Do you sometimes confuse Richard Wilbur, whose most anthologized poem is "Love Calls Us to the Things of This World," and Richard Hugo, whose most anthologized poem is "Degrees of Gray in Philipsburg"?

206. Are you for the glory or the fame?

207. Who decided Mark Strand's "Keeping Things Whole" should be his most anthologized poem?

208. What is a heroic couplet?

209. Do you consider *Sesame Street* or *Hill Street Blues* a greater poetic influence; *Rudolph the Red-Nosed Reindeer* or *The Deer Hunter*; *Purple Rain*, *The Color Purple*, or *The Color of Money*?

210. What kind of person looks to art to find history?

211. What kind of person looks to history to find the present?

212. Are Gil Scott-Heron's poems more or less important than his music?

213. Do you think all poets are spoken-word poets, or do you think all Black poets are spoken-word poets?

214. Where do poets like Pablo Neruda, Seamus Heaney, Wisława Szymborska, and Czesław Miłosz fit in your history?

215. Have you heard that reading a poem in translation is like chewing gum while it's in its wrapper?

216. Where does Derek Walcott go?

217. Is it better to be a poet of the blood or a poet of the mind?

218. Do you think that if trees could talk they would mostly talk about the weather?

219. What are your verbs?

220. Are you one of those people who confuse Nikky Finney and Nikki Giovanni?

End of Twentieth Century Examination, Part VIII?

The Tim Seibles Bookbioboardgame

Review of Tim Seibles's *Voodoo Libretto: New and Selected Poems*

Equipment

- Game board, constructed out of Ouija board and virtual pen and ink
- Encyclopedic Century Poet Magic Reversible card deck
- Tim Seibles charm (player piece)
- Dice

Dear Lucky Recipient

Congratulations, Tim Seibles fan!

You are receiving this very limited edition of our BOOKBIOBOARD-GAME for an extended reading of *Voodoo Libretto: New and Selected Poems*, by Tim Seibles, released in early 2022. Rereadings may be done alone or in pairs at your preferred light source and hour. A few members of our expert reading laboratory have reported enjoying the game best with Derridean deconstructions of the erotic in Tim Seibles. Our principles for enjoying the game are interchangeable with those of the *Frank O'Hara: Meditations in an Emergency Room and Board Game* and the *Bob Kaufman: Golden Sardine Eating Board Game*. But with Seibles we wanted to examine a classic midcentury Black baby boomer iron man work-a-day poet. Seibles is a poet who straddles our poetic past and future like Janus, the god of entrances and exits.

You are also receiving our Encyclopedic Century Poet Magic Reversible card deck. One side bears images of our extensive and ever-expanding collection of quintessential poets,* and one side is a slanting mystical tarot deck of poetry trivia, scholia, tidbits, and footnotes.

*We define *poet* as anyone who has ever written a true poem.

Introduction

TIM SEIBLES was born poised at the middle of the century between *Brown v. Board of Education* and the founding of Motown. Seibles was born in the year Emmett Till was murdered, one of the national shocks that set the Civil Rights era in motion. Tim Seibles was born at the birth of the civil and right. The proliferation of television meant a proliferation of images of horror at home and abroad. Tim Seibles was born at the birth of popular culture. His work is one measure of time. He came of age as political change slowly evolved into social change for Black people.

"The Word 1964–1981" from *Body Moves*, his 1988 debut, begins, "In Philadelphia / I went back to the school / we integrated. The bunch of us / had no idea how big a deal it was." The scene returns twenty-four years later in "Allison Wolff," from 2012's *Fast Animal*, a National Book Award finalist: "Was she Jewish? I was seventeen, / an 'Afro-American' senior transferred to a suburban school / that held just a few of us." The poem speaks in the register of memoir and the timbre of personal letters. The references to "the bunch of us" and "few of us" across the poems underscore the communal and cultural confidence encircling the racial interaction. In "Allison Wolff," "the monsters that murdered / Emmett Till—were they *everywhere*? / I didn't know. I didn't know enough." In the poem, Black nationalism tangles with integration. Freedom tangles with cultural solidarity. The poems are full of brothers, Black men and Black boys, Black fathers and sons, in earshot of Till's murder.

We encourage you to look closely at the measure of time in the body of work and in the body of Tim Seibles in America, and the spirit of his poems on earth.

Your Tim Seibles Charm

Make sure all poems have been experienced before assembly. Remove the Janus head and insert a watch battery (not included) beneath the hat. Assemble the parts of his grasp and reach first. The fingers are delicate. To prevent typos and bruises, do not use excessive force. Seibles belongs to a diminishing breed of troubadour poet, a tribe of bards and guitarists with agile, oversize hands, angular Thelonious Monk goatees, and smiles full of affectionate vocabularies. In *Body Moves*, the poem "The Snail" opens, "Sisters, / I am weak of your kisses / the wanting of them," announcing the images of mouths and kisses that will populate the poems. Seibles is a romantic.

Attach his vision to motion for enhanced visibility and mobility. Magical charms are attached to the touch of the poet, with (as Seibles writes in "Ode to My Hands") "each finger a cappella, singing / a song." The catalog of "lubricious dimensions" includes "women sailing the streets" before closing on two hands "an unreasonable world."

Once the lower and upper parts of the charm are connected, snap your fingers.

Play

This game demands careful emotional research before you actually start to play. There are no restrictions on how you may interpret the words. Once settled upon, you may shift your properties and opinions according to analysis and evidence.

Open your Encyclopedic Century Poet Magic Reversible card deck. Remove every African American poet born between Gwendolyn Brooks and Tim Seibles from the deck. Select untold influencer cards and untold peer cards. Shuffle each deck. Separate the deck of influencers into decks of family and books. Separate the deck of peers into decks of time and space. Shuffle each deck. Separate into decks of Blood, Muscle, Spirit, and Heart. Separate into decks of Reading, Writing, Speaking, and Singing. Shuffle each deck. Organize into decks of Life, Love, Music, and Place. These form the four draw piles and four routes to winning.

On your first turn, roll the dice and select which poets you want to influence the reading of which poems. The other player draws a card and invents a question about Tim Seibles. If you answer the question correctly you continue your turn by rolling the dice again.

Playing

Each of your turns concerns getting and placing new poets in conversation with Seibles. On your turn, try to fit your poet card to the Tim Seibles charm via reading, writing, or reciting. But be careful: winning battles will depend on vision, technique, and risk. You draw the card of Wanda Coleman and it is Black History Month in Ohio at the Rainbow Conference. You sit with Tim Seibles listening to Coleman's poems and bangles. You draw Michael S. Harper, and Harper's poetry collection *Dear John, Dear Coltrane* (1970) appears levitating above the game board. You sit with Tim at Cave Canem listening to Harper hold court. Sometimes you imagine Tim Seibles touring Coltrane's home as a teenager in Philly. Or you walk the campus of Old Dominion. Virginia is a land of poised and curious Black people.

If the interior and exterior are unevenly matched, you will still have an exciting game excursion. But when all is balanced, all is changed.

Strategy

Fans, in *Voodoo Libretto* you encounter the inner and outer realms of a work-a-day poet. While an undashed *workaday* can mean "commonplace," the hyphens in *work-a-day* restore the extraordinary work/labor involved in maintaining any sort of work/practice. This is a poet who works his days into poetry. *Voodoo Libretto*'s three hundred pages contain the frequencies and multitudes of Tim Seibles's life in poems. One way to have a winning reading experience involves placing Seibles's poems along a spectrum of personal and public history. Tim Seibles situates his life within a narrative of contemporary American culture. His poems narrate our common humanity and highlight what is uncommon about the commonplace and what is extraordinary about the ordinary. Seibles's voice in the poems has the inflections of memoirist and journalist mixed with bluesy avuncular troubadour. The result is a feeling of natural experience. Our aim is to stimulate that feeling in your reading of the poems. This very limited edition of THE TIM SEIBLES BOOKBIOBOARDGAME positions Seibles as a key to understanding the importance of poets who simply go about the work of a poet each day.

Winning the Game

When a player enters another poetic dimension, the game is over, and the reader may take the magic card deck to another book of poems or reshuffle for a new game with *Voodoo Libretto*.

Sample Board Game Recap

I played the following creatively improvised game against my shadow. (The shadow makes a Janus of the self.) It was all about poetry and probability, and I was pretty sure I was going to lose trying to read between the lines. I wanted to ponder the relationship between Bob Kaufman and Seibles, but I never drew the Bob Kaufman card. I never got to meditate on Seibles and Essex Hemphill. Or Seibles and Lynda Hull, both of whom spent time in Provincetown. This mercurial current edition of the magic card deck has a shortage of experimental poets, though all true poets are experimentalists. Most of the poets outside the old-fashioned literary canon are overlooked or undervalued, hideous or simply hiding out. I was happy to think about Seibles and several women poets in this game. I'm still thinking about Seibles, the erotic, and Audre Lorde. Several of the cards I drew are not included here. Nor is evidence of the tie-breaking extended couplet playoff overtime round against my shadow. I won by rhyming *hideous* and *hideout*.

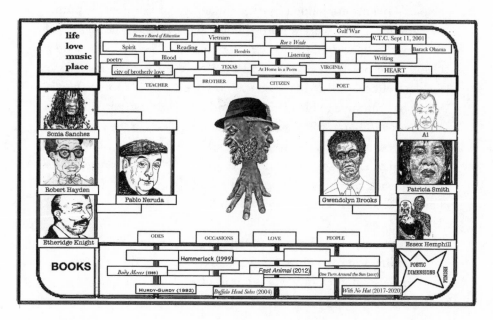

Books

The title of Seibles's first book, *Body Moves*, is taken from a Theodore Roethke poem. Roethke won a Pulitzer the year before Seibles was born, but he is mostly remembered now for a few poems: "My Papa's Waltz," "The Waking," and "Elegy for Jane," the last stanza of which begins:

If only I could nudge you from this sleep,
My maimed darling, my skittery pigeon.
Over this damp grave I speak the words of my love

Roethke's poems are lyrical technical wonders belonging to a white, masculine canon of modern American poetry. His gifts to the American poetry tradition—e.g., the gift of expressive humanity—have diminished as other, more expressive humanities deepen the waters of poetic literary history.

But Tim Seibles knows that Roethke's gifts remain relevant and influential. Seibles extends the tradition of witness in his debut collection. His interests are more carnal than political, honestly. And rightly. Seibles's poems are guided by the imperative of the poet to simply pay attention. The work absorbs bodies and personas, the sounds of the city, the television, the imagination. In his collection *Hammerlock* (1999), the poem "Kerosene," written after the LA riots, is a classic Seibles political poem: "In my country the weather / it's not too good." His books continue to blend political and social witness, particularly in *Buffalo Head Solos* (2004) and *Fast Animal*. Seibles is in the poetic gym every day. The poems magnify moments of reflection, nostalgia, and uncertainty. The tragically underread great poet Nin Andrews wrote the following blurb, which appears on the back of *Buffalo Head Solos* but also describes Seibles's body of work as a whole:

> In this mystical, romantic, and political collection, Seibles is willing to take a chance, any chance to engage the general malaise of our times. He is a musician of the spirit and of the body.

Reading

(Gwendolyn Brooks and Sonia Sanchez Cards Drawn Back-to-Back)

Seibles's classic poem "Trying for Fire" feels as if it's partly in dialogue with the Gwendolyn Brooks poem "a song for the front yard." Both poems announce Blackness through subtext rather than subject. Brooks could be speaking from her memory of sheltered girlhood desires: "A girl gets sick of a rose." But the poem's present-tense narration heightens the persona: "I'd like to be a bad woman, too." The sexual body takes priority over the Black body; without the white gaze there is no need to distinguish the color of bodies. The great "Poem at Thirty" from Sonia Sanchez's debut *Homecoming* (1969) is an intensification of Brooks's girlhood innocence. Brooks's daydream becomes nightmare as the girl from the front yard sleepwalks two miles. Sanchez ends by addressing a Black man in a gesture of solidarity and love: "here is my hand. / i am not afraid / of the night." *Homecoming* debuts when Seibles is fourteen. Seibles writes from the hinge of American civil upheaval and utopia. Write a poem for your personal utopia. Fill it with ghosts and muses.

Pablo Neruda

PABLO NERUDA

Among the poets he admires, Seibles reserves a special place for Pablo Neruda. We observe in Seibles's work not Neruda's political-social imperatives but rather the poet's sensuality and vitality. Each poet's work is underpinned by a strong, distinctive, and relatively simple sense of what matters in life—without being neutral to ethical and political contexts. If you consider yourself a true fan of Pablo Neruda, you likely know the poems found easily online. You know the best of the flowery odes and sonnets, and the Neruda classic "Me Gustas Cuando Callas" ("I Like for You to Be Still"). The title could be a hashtag for the patriarchal subtext of silencing, disappearing, erasing a woman. The title could also be a hashtag for the spiritual quiet associated with the addressee: "I like for you to be at rest." In "Love Sonnet XI," Neruda writes, "I crave your mouth, your voice, your hair." The second-person address qualifies any poem as lyric, says the critic Northrop Frye. Neruda's intimate direct address translates across language. The recipient of the poet's address tilts genre between prayer and poem. Try a contradictory love poem. List three wonderful details about the addressee, contradicting each with a conjunction such as *but*. For example: "I love the black ropes and tassels of your hair, but not the strands lingering like a child's cursive in our tub." Then list at least three unusual, even irritating details about the addressee, making them celebratory statements with a conjunction such as *and*. For example: "The whole house fills with the sound of your nose-blowing and even that crooked trumpeting has become a form of contentment." Use the prompts and your own ideas of contradictory love impulses to compose the poem.

Music

Tim Seibles's debut, *Body Moves*, is published in 1988, the year Michael Jackson's *Bad* album is played along with Prince's *Lovesexy* in some households. A heart has four chambers for love. Michael Jackson and Prince were born in 1958, three years after Tim Seibles. Does Seibles see the brothers as peers or influences?

Write the poet to commission poems about Prince, Michael Jackson, Teena Marie, John Coltrane.

Books

Nin Andrews's observation of the mystical in Seibles is acute. The work is mystical in the way Roethke's is mystical. As if a slight breathing and shifting presence is in the rooms and bushes. Seibles's poem "At 41" looks back on an idyllic childhood: the boy stands at the kitchen window watching his older brother and father going to catch the bus. In "Late Shift," the last poem in *Buffalo Head Solos*, he is still at that window of memory: "Where I am now / it's later . . . I have seen the door that is not there / still open."

The mystical can be found in the "caravan of clouds" in the poem "4 A.M.," from *Fast Animal*, in which couplets about a mystified birth join couplets about waking alone after a strange dream. Poems such as "Notes from Big Brah, Tom the Bomb," "Terry Moore," and "Donna James"—as well as the fine "Delores Jepps," not included in my edition of *Voodoo Libretto*—blend ode and elegy, celebrating and longing for friends and kin. The sensual physical imagery of the early poems gives way to metaphysical inflections in the later work. The poems are haunted by uncertainty. Jacket copy for *One Turn around the Sun* (2017) underlines the book's attempt "to define the first appearances of life's twilight." One bridge between *Fast Animal* and *One Turn* is the villanelle. The earlier book's "Mad Poets Villanelle" evolves into the later book's blues villanelles: "Taste Me Blues Villanelle," "Zombie Blues Villanelle," "Thirty-Thirty Blues Villanelle." His foray into the form offers basic definitive evidence of his ongoing practice of poetic risk, poetic workout, exercises toward emotional and spiritual fortitude. Seibles continues pursuing a perfection of the form. The blues villanelle requires rhyme, refrain, and turns of phrase, effusive expression of vernacular rhetoric. A rhetoric of expressive conversation, a conversion of nouns to verbs, vice to aversion, and vice versa—a poem to make the mind more self-contesting and fine.

Reading

After reading Tim Seibles's poems "At 41," "At 59," and "Poem at 64," ruminate on the ways Seibles engages Martin Heidegger's theory of time. When reading any two lines in one of the poems, part of you must appear in a mirror. You will win double points for answering trivia questions bordering on privacy and secrecy. Describe the poet's brother by reading between the lines. The parts of you in the city of family, friends, and lovers are divided between yesterday and tomorrow. The liturgies of longing issuing from the part of you facing a window are less blue than the liturgies of longing issuing from the part of you facing a widow.

Romance

Tim Seibles is a romantic. His early poems contend with flesh and longing; his late poems contend with mortality and desire. "Heidegger argues that time does not find its meaning in eternity, time finds its meaning in death," writes Lilian Alweiss in "Heidegger and 'The Concept of Time.'" Seibles's time finds meaning in the lines creasing the poem and the body. Take a day with three poems about aging, a perfect and exact record of human intimacy, humanity, and philosophy. Ruminate on the ways they tackle time.

Love

Tim Seibles has you pondering a definition of the erotic poem—versus, say, the love poem, the sexual poem. Charles Bukowski has a few skeezy sex poems. For more vivid poems about fucking, see Wanda Coleman's debut, *Mad Dog Black Lady* (1979), written during her tenure at a porn magazine in the 1970s. Pondering the erotic poem may lead you to a carnal zone or a psychic one. You may end up consulting Audre Lorde's notion of the erotic, particularly her essay "Uses of the Erotic: The Erotic as Power":

> The very word *erotic* comes from the Greek word *eros*, the personification of love in all its aspects—born of Chaos, and personifying creative power and harmony. When I speak of the erotic, then, I speak of it as an assertion of the life-force of women; of that creative energy empowered, the knowledge and use of which we are now reclaiming in our language, our history, our dancing, our loving, our work, our lives.

Audre Lorde has you pondering the aspects of the feminine in *Voodoo Libretto*. What aspects of the feminine Lorde describes are present in Tim Seibles's new volume of poetry? What aspects of the feminine Lorde describes are present in the work of *any* heterosexual male poet exploring the erotic?

Music

The talking Tim Seibles charm quotes Theodore Roethke's poem "In a Dark Time": "What's madness but nobility of soul / At odds with circumstance?" If you are playing along you may choose this moment to highlight signs of madness in the lines of Seibles's body of work. The madness will seem like a casual kind of ecstasy in the early work. The madness of "The Kiss," the madness of "Trying for Fire," and of "Kerosene." In "Mad Poets Villanelle," Seibles repeats, "I think I know why certain poets go mad." The Seibles charm makes the madness into forms of music, anecdote, and beauty. Try your own blues villanelle.

Spirit

The way in which the geographical valley of a text—on the unfabricated, rather fragrant path to a body of language—affects the "what," "why," and "how" of seductively inhabiting this text, I want to lay on you like the lines of a couplet demarcating the upper and lower hemispheres surrounding us. Theodor Adorno writes that exile is a "life in suspension": being placed outside the body. Baby, your body is phenomenologically and ontologically fundamental and irreducible. Space and time are poetic inside and outside places because text is given texture between context and subtext. Do you believe being a stranger leads to empathy? ("Vocabulary Brother.")

Reading

Voodoo is an opera in three acts, with music and libretto by Harry Lawrence Freeman, that premiered in 1928. *Voodoo* is set in Louisiana during the Reconstruction era. A plantation servant and voodoo queen vie for the love of an overseer to a score of shouts, arias, tangos, gospel hymns, and voodoo dances. The first production since 1928 took place in 2015 in Harlem. How does this information reframe your reading of the volume of Tim Seibles's new and selected poems by the same name?

Trivia

Tim Seibles looks on the ethics of forgetting within a context of forgiving. Achilles's weakness was bipedal. Set threw Osiris into a coffin and then into the Nile. Jorge Luis Borges could be stimulated by literature, copulating over a well-wrought sentence before he became blind. Is it possible such a delicate arousal may never grace an adult again? ("Vocabulary Brother.")

Poetry

In late summer, the city installs a ten-foot Tim Seibles sculpture out-side the Poets' Vocational High School at an angle, to suggest his fingers are embedded in the earth like the roots of trees. Poised under a revolving hat, the expression of the poet is weightless. That fall, all the poets of the city enter the "Poems for the Tim Seibles Statue Contest." They wear and sell T-shirts saying "Let's Poet." This phrase turns a common noun, *poet*, into a verb, a rhetorical device known as *anthimeria*. For example: "The Rabbit turtled along the road to the Poets' Vocational High School." Anthimeria example number two: "The thunder would not peace at my bidding," says a young poet reading *King Lear* in the cafeteria. Wordsworth promised no prosopopoeia, the personification of abstract ideas, in his "Preface to *Lyrical Ballads*." Prosopopoeia and Anthimeria Jackson are sisters who collaborate on a poem about the Tim Seibles statue. One overcast morning, the principal poet carries the Jackson sisters' small tercet to the flagpole. A Tim Seibles poem will have you asking: If Phillis Wheatley published *Poems on Various Subjects, Religious and Moral* in 1773, and Samuel Taylor Coleridge then published *Poems on Various Subjects* in 1796, why not you?

Trivia

Only one poem by Tim Seibles, "Trying for Fire," is sandwiched between Primus St. John and Ntozake Shange in the Library of America's anthology *African American Poetry: 250 Years of Struggle and Song*, edited by Kevin Young (2020). The anthology is among the most comprehensive catalogs of African American poetry on record. Naturally, certain poets will have more work than others. Maybe one barometer for inclusion is implicit in the subtitle: poets expressing extraordinary struggle and/or extraordinary song. Doesn't *Voodoo Libretto* remind you of Seibles's particular struggle and song? Which poems would you include in a fully comprehensive edition of the anthology?

The Renegade Poetic Fortune-Telling Machine

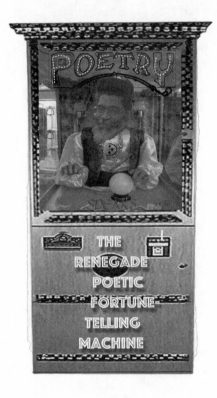

The legendary, one-of-a-kind Renegade Poetic Fortune-Telling Machine can be found near the boardwalks of Atlantic City, but you will need to read between the lines of *Ideas of Improvisation*, the first full-length poetry collection by Joel Dias-Porter, to locate it.

Like the poet himself, the figure inside the machine wears a black and gold wizard's robe with a Steelers logo on the chest and a tilted baseball cap. The Fortune Teller is made of the refurbished parts of a straightforward tape recorder, the motherboard of somebody's super-computer, a Cape Verdean's Volkswagen, miles and miles of speaker wire, an old-school slot machine, and a casino stool with a plush seat cushion.

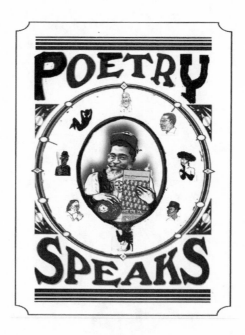

The contents of the machine (which has the same dimensions as Dr. Who's TARDIS Police Box) include: the fortune teller, his old-school records, a white disco crystal ball, a turntable, a cell phone, poker chips, tea bags, and the book *Ideas of Improvisation*. The latter is a Black man's collection of odes and meditations, full of poems decades in the making, which reveal the people dear to him: his muses and loves, his memories, testimonies, and allegories. The poem "Whitman's Sampler" reads:

Here, take this gift,
Which too long I was offering to feed my soul

This is the gift of a poet who has devoted his life to writing. The poems are not autobiographical in any typical way (and certainly not in the manner of a standard debut), instead conveying memories rooted in ideas of form and language. I think of Elizabeth Bishop writing and rewriting her poems in the long years between each book. The end product is not so much an autobiographical account as the document of an artistic process. These poems live in different forms at different moments in the poet's life; the hours put into them make them invaluable. Imagine a meal so amazing it would take twenty years to prepare.

The Renegade Poetic Fortune-Telling Machine offers The Tarot of Voices when it senses you are in need of conversation with other poets. When it comes up, your reading of *Ideas of Improvisation* will be guided by resonances ranging from Hughes's blues to Walt Whitman's wildness.

TAROT OF SISTERS

THE BASHŌ IN YOU

PEARL EARRING AMONG DREADLOCKS YOUR GRIN

Whatever your question, the Renegade Poetic Fortune-Telling Machine will spit out a tarot card, conjuring an answer for you. The Machine answers your questions in the subtextual threads of Dias-Porter's poems. Fragments of imagery and lyric flash in the text of each card. For example, the Tarot of Sisters card alerted me to the presence of Black women in *Ideas of Improvisation*. The Tarot of Sisters card prompted me to revisit "The Bashō in You," six surreal haiku-ish stanzas flashing with imagery of pistachios, ponytails, blackberry brandy. Inside the poem is the inner poem in red:

PEARL EARRINGS AMONG THE DREADLOCKS YOUR GRIN

The image emerges like a koanish snapshot of beauty. The dreadlocked smiling presence becomes muse and ghost across the book. "The Bashō in You" is an ode to haiku and desire. The tone here, and in many of the collection's poems, combines a sense of play and longing. I recalled the hair of women I loved as I read Dias-Porter's poem. I have received a different fortune, a new joy and insight every time I've read these poems.

TAROT OF MYSTERY

SEASCAPE WITH VESSEL
FOR CESÁRIA ÉVORA

AT THE END OF A WOMAN'S CIGARETTE
THE MYSTERY OF A GIRL

These poems are the meditations of a poet who has found his muses in music. The machine plays *Kind of Blue* some days. On other days Cesária Évora can be heard echoing through the piping. Birds and pigeons gather on the roof of the machine as it speaks haiku and sports scores on the hour.

The Tarot of Mystery and Tarot of Music cards may be drawn when you are in need of mobile solitude. Take the book and some headphones on a bus and travel overnight to your mother's home.

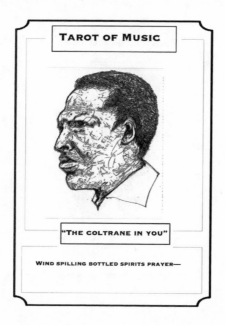

TAROT OF MUSIC

"THE COLTRANE IN YOU"

WIND SPILLING BOTTLED SPIRITS PRAYER—

"The Coltrane in You" is an ode to friendship and language. But there is another poem *inside* the poem, which reads:

WIND SPILLING BOTTLED SPIRITS PRAYER—

Inside a meditation on cultural experience is a quieter thread of personal experience. Inside the stillness is a renegade sensibility. Inside the mythic figures and historical contexts is an intimate wind spilling prayer.

TAROT OF MUSES

BETCHA BY GOLLY WOW
FOR PHYLLIS HYMAN

YOUR LIPS NAKED WITH JUNE RAIN.

I have been a fan and student of Joel Dias-Porter's work for my entire writing career. I consider him my brother and peer, my personal Walt Whitman, my lifelong friend and guide inside and outside poetry. I first heard Dias-Porter (whom I knew only as "Renegade" for almost half a decade!) read "Subterranean Night-Colored Magi" at the Associated Writing Programs Conference in Pittsburgh in 1995. All I recall of those three days (where some of the most established poets and writers took the main stage) is meeting Dias-Porter and seeing Renegade and his poets at the open mic. I'm not even sure *I* read at the open mic. Renegade blew an imaginary trumpet with his hands and mouth, performing what I can only describe as verbal acrobatics while reading a poem about Miles Davis. It was my first literary conference. I didn't belong there. I would have gone to hang with my rappers and basketball players if he hadn't invited me to hang with him and the other WritersCorp folks—a group of poets who were teaching in the schools and prisons around DC in the nineties. Renegade was already a friend or mentor to many young poets around the city, some of whom would become my lifelong friends and acquaintances: Yona Harvey, Ta-Nehisi

Coates, Douglas Kearney, Amaud Jamaul Johnson, Jeffrey McDaniel, A. Van Jordan. In one way or another, I know all these poets because of Joel Dias-Porter.

You'd have to speak with professors, poets, teachers, bookstore clerks, students, poker players, law professors, jazz musicians, cashiers, and bus drivers to know all the poet formerly known as DJ Renegade has done as a poet. His IMDB page notes that he was born and raised in Pittsburgh, worked as a professional DJ in DC, and competed in the National Poetry Slam from 1994 to 1999. It also lists many of the places his poetry, jazz music, and performances have appeared—from *TIME* magazine and *The Washington Post* to BET and *The Today Show*—and mentions that Renegade was named the Haiku Slam Champion in both 1998 and '99.

The Carnegie Library's website's listing of famous Pittsburghers once included the following "haiku-like poems," which had been spray-painted behind the outfield wall of Forbes Field:

FROZEN ROPE PAST FIRST
ROBERTO SCOOPS AND RIFLES
DUST SWIRLS, UMP PUNCHES

FLY ARCS HIGH TO RIGHT
CLEMENTE BASKET CATCHES
ADIOS AMIGO.

The website goes on to name the poems' author as "the poet identi-fied only as . . . DJ RENEGADE."

TAROT OF HEROES

EL MAGNIFICO

THE SOUND OF PRAYING WHICH IS OUR WINDOW

"El Magnifico," Dias-Porter's elegy for Roberto Clemente, combines the folk mythos of the John Henry figure and the intimate lamentation of lost fathers. The Tarot of Heroes card reads:

THE SOUND OF PRAYING WHICH IS OUR WINDOW

The poems create an archive of arts and athletes as surrogate father figures. Sons and fathers hear themselves in the "our." The sound of praying emanates from mouths and music.

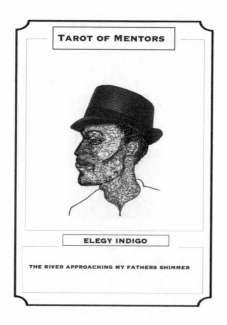

TAROT OF MENTORS

ELEGY INDIGO

THE RIVER APPROACHING MY FATHERS SHIMMER

The Renegade Poetic Fortune-Telling Machine may offer Tarot of Heroes or Tarot of Mentors to remind you the ghosts are real: "Finally, finally, I come to believe in loss as a way of knowing," Dias-Porter writes in "Elegy Indigo." When one of these cards comes up in your tarot reading, be prepared to be guided by ghosts.

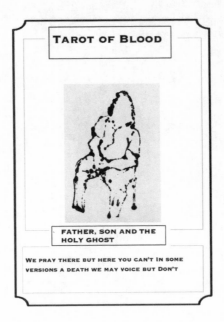

TAROT OF BLOOD

FATHER, SON AND THE HOLY GHOST

WE PRAY THERE BUT HERE YOU CAN'T IN SOME
VERSIONS A DEATH WE MAY VOICE BUT DON'T

Whatever your problem or dilemma, a poem from *Ideas of Improvisation* will have your answer. The book doubles as a poetic diary filling the reader with the life of the poet. The Tarot of Blood leads the reader to an elegy: "Father, Son, and the Holy Ghost." Inside the poem, another poem rests in red font:

> WE PRAY THERE BUT HERE YOU CAN'T IN SOME
> VERSIONS A DEATH WE MAY VOICE BUT DON'T

The thread of dark red words weaves a quieter, shyer spirit inside the linguistic swagger of the surrounding text. The Tarot of Blood forecasts a raw, vulnerable encounter with *Ideas of Improvisation*. When this card comes up before your reading, the poems will lead you to the answers within. Be very still, and listen . . .

TAROT OF LONGING

AN IDEA OF IMPROVISATION AS COMPULSIVE PRAYER

BLACK LIPSTICK A CLARINET HER ROSARY

Ideas of Improvisation fills the reader with renegade psyche. It captures the poet's dreams and fantasies. The poems are tarots of longing for people, odes and compulsive prayers for romantic company. Dias-Porter's style carries echoes of the soul crooner and traveling troubadour. His visions and revisions maintain a constant pulse of Romantic desire. A Pablo Nerudan love frames the book. The poet is a blues haikuist and a lovelorn monk of the dictionary and jukebox both.

If you cannot find a Poetic Fortune-Telling Machine, find the book of poems, *Ideas of Improvisation*. A book for lovers seeking repair but never revenge. For mothers wondering after eccentric sons, for sons wondering after nomadic fathers, for fathers and loners and gamblers and all us eccentric, wondering spirits of the present unsettled world. The book holds poems written and rewritten, retitled and reconfigured, forgotten then revised several times over many decades, creating the poetic equivalent of a very fine Johnny Walker Blue for the mind and mouth.

You must read the poems to discover your fortune. Your payment for this vintage new age mercurial clairvoyant poetry is simply the price of the book.

Brigit Pegeen Kelly and the Case of the Missing Manuscript! (1951–2016)

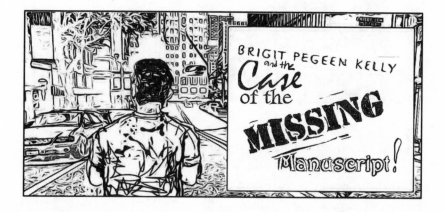

Calling all Poetic Detectives!

Since Brigit Pegeen Kelly became eternal poetry in October 2016, have you had dreams concerning the poems she wrote in the twelve years between 2004's *The Orchard* and her passing?

Embark on a poetic mystery reading body language and figures of speech. Your first clue: the manuscript is likely portable and shaped like several layers of paper-thin doors opening on more doors.

Your dream is to locate the manuscript of poems. Detection without intrusion consists of reading *The Orchard, Song,* and *To the Place of Trumpets*, noting animals and the traces they leave behind. For example, a scorpion and the flame it becomes when magnified. Search the riverbank, the pond, and the lake for water under the bridge.

When you come to the farm once inhabited by the mysterious poet, you will be asked to depart.

Return to your hotel by the highway looking for clues.

In a fine obituary, the late Eavan Boland mused on Kelly's enigmatic living presence and the quiet of her death. Boland discusses the uncollected Kelly poem, "Closing Time; Iskandariya." I saw Kelly read at the same Breadloaf reading Eavan Boland recalls hearing "Closing Time; Iskandariya" in the obituary. Or I dreamed it. I saw her once at the KGB reading series on the Lower East Side of New York City. We also spent some time together teaching at a conference in Bloomington, Indiana, near where she grew up. She was a magical presence. We talked about the dark spiritual genius of Sylvia Plath.

As a poetic detective, you will have to decide in which location (the fallow part of the orchard, the fox hole, the deer heart) the book may be hidden and attempt writing the poem Kelly may have written to corroborate the hypothesis.

Stop at the gas stations along the route to your hotel and recite "Closing Time; Iskandariya" to the customers and workers you meet. A clue can be found in the following section:

> In truth, it is shy, the scorpion, a creature with eight
> eyes and almost no sight, who shuns the daylight, and
> is driven mad by fire, who favors the lonely spot, and
> feeds on nothing much, and only throws out its poison
> barb when backed against a wall—a thing like me,
> but not the thing I asked for, a thing, by accident or
> design, I am now attached to.

Walk into the woods behind the gas stations at the hour the wolf and dog wear the same shadow. The figure of a statue is whatever you can imagine—a classical torso from a Rilke poem, a man on a horse, a centaur.

The statue can be found in a garden of the apocalypse, of Eden, of wonderland: whatever you can imagine. Your choices result in different paths to the missing poems. Look for the poems in the fields you pass along the highway to and from the farm, the maze of animal dust and shadow. Her people and ghosts will ask you to depart. In the field near the farm get down on your belly like a scorpion and sleep dreaming of Kelly in the mouth of a dragon for awhile. Walk into a strange town and fall asleep on the steps of the library, dreaming of Kelly in the mouth of a dragon cradling a dragon. Search the dream for the missing clue or enter the unlit library. Read the blank pages with a magnified vision, read the lines written on the torso in invisible ink. Look for the next clue to the great poet's missing poems.

Guan Guan,
1929-2021

Inside the very tall building full of offices and playrooms and laboratories full of mathematicians, magicians, witch doctors, astrologists, alchemists, scientists, and their assistants, a very old woman told me the office of the elder poet was on the top floor. The best years of my life were already behind me. I had been a fool in love. I had been a fool to love. I had been a fool with love, most importantly. If there was time, I'd ask the elder poet whether I'd be lucky enough to be a fool again. But first I planned to ask what would happen to my son. He was growing into a man. What if he had no father to teach him to talk with policemen or teachers. The elder began telling me a story before I could ask anything. "An emperor wanted to know his future. Knowledge, like everything else in our world, was rooted in magic." The poet said, "The emperor wanted to foresee his oversights, his downfall, his undoing; he wanted to know his future betrayers." The elder poet began

vibrating. His cell phone was ringing somewhere in the folds of his robe. I made my way back through the waiting room. You know who was waiting there. The doors of the lone elevator were broken coming and going. A shaft of darkness encased in shafts of light. I was told writing gave us power over the past. That language and time were fundamentally connected. That one who arrives too late is too careless with time just as one who arrives too early is too careful with it.

TWENTIETH CENTURY EXAMINATION

Part IX: What Grows Harder to See as You Get Closer to It?

221. Were there any teachers who had a particularly strong influence on your life?

222. Who and where were you when Derek Walcott won the Nobel Prize in Literature in 1992?

223. Who had a tomboy neighbor named Wild Iris long before reading Louise Glück's *Wild Iris*?

224. Was the poem Maya Angelou read at Bill Clinton's swearing in titled "On the Pulse of Morning" or "On the Pulse of Mourning"?

225. If you own a copy of the 1993 *Pittsburgh Book of Contemporary American Poetry,* can you imagine the anthology's book party attended by the great Sharon Olds; the motorcycle-riding, leather-jacketed Larry Levis; the new ghost of Etheridge Knight; Afaa Weaver when he went by Michael and was fresh from the Maryland mills; Carol Muske-Dukes when she went by Carol Ann with an eye on Levis; Ted Kooser in his insurance man's tie; and Belle Waring wearing a nurse's white?

226. Does your view of a poem change the longer you look at it?

227. Should I say I also imagine two of my best teachers, Toi Derricotte and Betsy Sholl, chatting somewhere at this book party?

228. If a young white poet raised in the Deep South by a father who names the family dog a racial slur writes an elegy about the father in your poetry class, is the young white poet allowed to include the name of the dog?

229. Do you ever wonder whether W. H. Auden's poem "September 1, 1939," which says about the German invasion of Poland, "The unmentionable odor of death / Offends the September night," was circulated after the September 11 attacks because it spoke to the occasion or because *September* was in the title?

230. Do your actual teachers matter more than what you learn in books or music or movies?

231. What is the likeliest effect of poetry on the quality of public schools?

232. Would you believe I once saw Robert Frost reincarnated as a black bear vomiting clouds of bees and honey on a road near his farm?

233. Does all history end and begin with your musing?

234. What if you are playing a Black middle-aged present-day high school AP English teacher who wakes from dream to dream?

235. Who cares about an American poem?

236. Ed Robeson and Thylias Moss are part of what literary movement?

237. Is the number of people who wounded you bigger or smaller than the number of people you have wounded?

238. What was your favorite childhood meal?

239. What was your grandmother doing at the hour of your birth?

240. Remember what happened when Lucille Clifton published *Blessing the Boats*?

241. Who remembers what happened after Amiri Baraka, at the time New Jersey poet laureate, hooted *who who who* in the smoke of the Twin Towers?

242. Would you agree that the price you pay for telling the truth is never as high as the price you pay for telling a lie?

243. If you are wounded but still missing the point of something, couldn't the tear become infected with fear or stupidity?

244. Shouldn't a rip in the spirit you wear be thoughtfully repaired?

245. Isn't learning healing?

246. When did you last sing to someone?

247. What does the poet love more than poems, and hate more than hate and death; what does the poet among all tribes of poets, and the poet alone with the self, desire; what if not art is a weapon for eternity?

248. What are three warnings you have received?

249. What's the answer to a question you might have asked yourself ten years ago?

250. What's the question you may still ask yourself ten years from now?

251. Can we devise some ideas about what's been going on these last twenty years, if we tally up what's been going on the last hundred or so, or no?

252. Which matters most: the poem, the poet, or the state of poetry?

253. What is a rhetorical question?

254. How are you feeling?

255. Do you have your answers ready?

Temporary End of Examination

The African Rainbow Lizard

1. In Pompano, Black people are descendants of the African rainbow lizard. Native to Africa, the eggs of the lizard were stored in the hair of kidnapped Africans. I have no information regarding why it carries a rainbow, having seen the losses it saw on slave ships and coasts.

2. At cookouts, a single African rainbow lizard is guaranteed to appear on the picnic table among the hot dogs, ribs, store-bought coleslaw, and canned sodas.

3. Some African rainbow lizards possess a heightened taste in music, cinema, and art. Others have a gift for reading people. The African rainbow lizard can survive on a diet of fire ants and fireflies, pill bugs and ladybugs, houseflies, houseplants.

And Mother's Day flowers.

4. Some Black working-middle-class parents work too much to attend the games and performances of their Black working-middle-class children. At night the parents are exhausted and temperamental, pepper and salt shakes from them like sweat. They worked themselves to death, naturally. In Pompano Beach I saw folk black as beetles and I saw a Black child place a beetle in his mouth. I saw roaches large as matchboxes. I saw Black folk cuss and joke with smoke in the mouth. "*Agama agama*," I heard them whisper. "*Agama agama*, the African rainbow lizard."

5. Outside of Pompano about a mile from the sea, where the annual African rainbow lizard convention convenes, an actual African rainbow lizard has never been seen. A number of elderly Black folk and their grandchildren attend. No one is allowed to mention the African rainbow lizard when the annual African rainbow lizard convention convenes. Instead the elderly Black folk tell fish fables.

6. The largest and most powerful African rainbow lizards are often cannibalistic, devouring their young, according to page 174 of V. A. Harris's *The Life of the Rainbow Lizard* (1964).

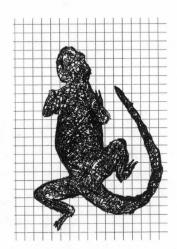

7. The African rainbow lizard often runs a small business. The mother runs a hair salon out of the house. The father runs a fish market. When he drives Black Pompano in his beat-up pickup, coming and going, someone shouts his name. Fish guts slush in the buckets, fish guts gush the air with disgust. But men cheer him when he drives. Women wear hair elaborately weaved, pressed and styled by the mother.

8. African rainbow lizards do not have white people for bosses.

9. To witness the sad and beautiful changes in a family is just about reason enough to live.

10. I was not an African rainbow lizard. Their cousin wasn't my real father. None of their blood was in me. Each summer I lived fearing this would be revealed to them.

11. If a lizard can talk, it is guaranteed to sing beautifully.

12. I saw someone stumbling in the doorway. No, two men hugging, tussling, breathing. The mother was screaming *Agama, agama*. The father's tongue was like the forked, vicious tongue of the African rainbow lizard. He seemed to be trying to bite into the neck of his son. Kiss him, lick him, I might have slept through the scene, overhearing a dream, not the mother screaming as she bites her lip and wields a knife at the son or perhaps the father, not the mother, but several of the daughters screaming "Mama, Mama," but it sounded like *Agama, agama*.

13. Or they are joking how the father died clenching a nickel. Several bundles of twenty-dollar bills rolled in his church socks drawer, another bundle of tens under his deathbed and pillow, a couple pounds of mason jars full of coins in his closet, the little quarter-ounce nugget of silver he found when digging the grave of his father tucked safely in his mouth, all of it, stinking like the guts of fish. The clothes washed twice a day, twice a week, and stinking still. The socks balled tight in his drawer beside the money and pistol stunk of fish, the scales of several varieties of fish were under his bed and nails, tiny greasy granular scales glimmered in his hair, his pillow stunk of fish. The mother worked herself to death. The father died with his fist balled so tightly no one could say whether it was money or scales he clenched.

A Poetics of Practice Keynote

Once, during a Q and A, a woman in the audience asked if I was poetic because I'd been a basketball player. I understood the question. As you might guess, I played basketball all through school and college. Though she couldn't have known it, I often use basketball as an analogy for my poetics. Practice matters more than the game in sports. To excel at anything you have to spend more time in practice than in the game. If you are not practicing when you are not in the game, you don't really love the game. I maintain a regular writing practice where, as in basketball practice, winning isn't the point. Thus, nor is losing. I once did a 360 dunk in practice. Because I was practicing at it. Took maybe two or three attempts. I never did it in a game, though, if you see my point. If practice is about the glory, and the game is about the fame, I'm for the glory. "Practice" is the point of an art practice. At the root of *practice* is *praxis*, which is Greek for "doing." My essential poetics is simply to be doing something, making something, playing, struggling, learning something. Practice and poetics are synonymous in my mind. Both are enhanced by variation: particularness, adaptability as well as resistance. I want to sweat. I maintain a basic poetics of practice.

But that is not how I heard the question. Were my poems poetic because I'd played basketball? She moved her arms back and forth in a running motion as she asked it. She was trying to be kind; she was trying to draw connections. The smell of cliché almost overpowered the smell of racism beneath it. Racists, when they are passive, don't bother me too much. Ignorant racists (not the same as passive racists) concern me only when they are in power. The poems I'd read that evening were maybe, if it can be reduced, exploring a poetics (a practice) of kinds and kindness: kinds of sonnets, kinds of Americans, kinds of time, kinds of assassins; the power of love versus the power of unkindness. Unkindness is a bit more nuanced than hate. Unkindness suggests the opposite of generosity, which is a bit sadder than mere hate. Unkindness suggests the opposite of consideration, which is a poverty of thoughtfulness. One who does not "consider before acting" is inconsiderate. One who does not treat others as he would like to be treated is inconsiderate. At the root of *selfish*, the noun *self* suggests a consideration for little more than the self. At the root of *kindness*, the noun *kind* suggests groups, types, character. The nice white woman's stupid, racist, cliché question essentially suggested I was a certain kind of poet because I appeared to be a certain kind of Black man. Obviously, she was wrong.

But she was also kind of right. And in any case, isn't it kind of true that everything a brother or sister does is poetic because Blackness is inherently, existentially, essentially poetic? Black people's "Blackness" is poetic. This is not the same as saying poetics are equal to Blackness. There are many varieties of "poetic." There are poetic styles and styles of poetics. All language is poetic. To say Blackness is poetic is to say the history of Black people in America is both a poetic story and a story of Black folk's poetics.

Lots of brilliant Black people have written about the poetry in Black people. Gwendolyn Brooks made a life doing it. She never left Chicago, the place she grew up; she wrote about everything she saw in Chicago. Obviously, she saw a lot of Black people. The pool players in "We Real Cool" are, according to the backstory, Black. And yet, she never mentions it in the poem. Sometimes she's so Black she doesn't have to say anything about it. After I read her poem "The Mother" my freshman year in college, I decided I'd become a poet. I wept reading it. I'd gotten my high school girlfriend pregnant. I'd never talked to anyone about it; not even the girl and I really talked about it. But there it was in her poem. It is also a poem that does not mention "Blackness." Except it was written by a Black woman. The poem makes a profound and human impact even when you know nothing about the author. That's the power of language. But should you happen to have been raised by a Black woman and then learn a Black woman wrote the poem, well, that means something. It pretty much means anything is possible. Where does a poet like Gwendolyn Brooks, born in 1917, at the start of the Great Migration, to a janitor and schoolteacher who moved the family to Chicago a month after Brooks's birth, come from? I want to read you a sentence from her Wikipedia page bio: "Due to the social dynamics of the various schools, in conjunction with the era in which she attended them, Brooks faced much racial injustice. Over time, this experience helped her understand the prejudice and bias in established systems and dominant institutions, not only in her own surroundings but in every relevant American mindset." We all kind of know what that means, but why is it worded so inoffensively, a jargon of niceties? One cannot really say where Brooks comes from. Except to say she comes from an effusive, natural Blackness. And Womanness. I saw my mother in "The Mother." I saw that girlfriend in "The Mother."

I was never a poetic basketball player. Though I've been this tall since I was fifteen, I was not tough, graceful, or naturally talented. I was thin as a bow; half-blind. But I practiced enough to get a basketball scholarship—it's the only way I could have gone to college. I practiced enough to look like the sort of Black man the white woman saw. Let us assume then, yes, there is a poetics of Blackness. Black people share a historical and constant relationship to freedom. Black people should not exist. You may already know my mother had me when she was sixteen. I mention it all the time. If she could have afforded an abortion, she would have had one. I mention it all the time because no one ever imagined I'd live, certainly not make a living telling you about it. And so here I am, being inherently poetic. I need only tell the story of a Black man who is alive. It is a poetics, a practice of bearing witness: simply showing up, simply sharing. Is anyone who is born Black born a poet? If your answer is yes, you are on the side of the white woman. Is anyone born Black born tragic? I don't think so. Is anyone born Black born beautiful? Maybe.

Kindness is harder than you might imagine. Being Black in many cases gives me the right to be unkind. A poetics of Blackness gives me the right to reprimand, in almost any manner I prefer, a white woman who tries to reduce my story to a cliché. No friend of mine would blame me for being inconsiderate to an ignorant question. But kindness takes practice. Moreover, seeing things "one way" is just not good existential practice. I work to expand the compassion in my poetics. You may have already realized, I take Gwendolyn Brooks as a model in this approach to writing and living. I want to give a shout-out to the spectacles, speculations, and especially perceptive speculativeness of Gwendolyn Brooks. When pressed and dressed up like an honor roll student at the Pulitzer awards, she was not diminished. When the rebel Black Arts poets arrived chanting and crying at her door in Chicago, she let them in, she called them children, she grew out her afro. When she passed the Black boys in the pool halls and shadows, and basketball courts and courthouses, she spoke to them. We are still listening. To the notion of inherent poetic Blackness, she adds a notion of kindness. It is not niceness. Niceness is superficial, civil, cosmetic. Kindness is closer to the bone; truth is in the marrow of kindness. Even a vulgar kindness, a selfish kindness; one can offer a cruel kindness—truth can be a kind of cruel kindness. I didn't embarrass the woman. I gave a slanted nod and asked what she meant.

Acknowledgments

My sincere thanks to the editors and staff of the following publications for first acknowledging the poems (and previous versions of the poems) in this manuscript:

"The African Rainbow Lizard" appeared in *Haunt Journal of Art*.

"Barbara Chase-Riboud," "Bob Kaufman," "Essex Hemphill," "Mari Evans," "Reginald Shepherd," "Russell Atkins," "Sonia Sanchez," and "William Waring Cuney" appeared in *The Baffler*.

"Between Practice" appeared in *Bodies Built for Game: The Prairie Schooner Anthology of Contemporary Sports Writing*, edited by Natalie Diaz.

"Everyday Mojo Letters to Yusef," "Michael S. Harper," and "Lynda Hull" appeared in *Boston Review*.

"Everyday Mojo Letters to Yusef" also appeared in *Dear Yusef: Essays, Letters, and Poems for and about One Mr. Komunyakaa*, edited by John Murillo and Nicole Sealey.

"A Lucille Clifton–Inspired Sterling Brown Teaching Fable" appeared in *Michigan Quarterly Review*.

"My Gwendolyn Brooks" appeared in the Poetry Society Annual Lecture Series and *The Poetry Review*.

"The Nine Muses of a Poetry Enthusiast's View Of History or the Nine Multi-faced, Multifaceted Muses of American Poetic Production? (Twentieth Century Examination, Key I)," "Reflections and Foresight upon a Century of Poetry, 2016," and "Twentieth Century Examination" with illustrations appeared in *The Hopkins Review*.

"A Poetics of Practice Keynote" appeared in *Furious Flower: Seeding the Future of African American Poetry*, edited by Joanne V. Gabbin and Lauren K. Alleyne.

"Poetry Foundation Journal Days, 2006" appeared on the Poetry Foundation website (www.poetryfoundation.org) and was republished in *How We Do It: Black Writers on Craft, Practice, and Skill*, edited by Jericho Brown and Darlene Taylor.

A prose version of "Twentieth Century Examination" appeared as the 2019 Blaney Lecture for the Academy of American Poets.

"The Renegade Poetic Fortune-Telling Machine" and "The Tim Seibles Bookbioboardgame" appeared in *The Yale Review*.

"Snow for Wallace Stevens" is reprinted from *Lighthead*.

"Wallace Stevens Key" appeared in *jubilat*.

"The Wicked Candor of Wanda Coleman" appeared in *The Paris Review*.

Drawing for "My Gwendolyn Brooks" with credit to Jill Krementz; Timeline Drawing of Audre Lorde with credit to photographer Robert Alexander; Timeline Drawing of Octavia E. Butler with credit to photographer Miriam Berkley.

My gratitude for the support of Blue Flower Arts, New York University, and the John D. and Catherine T. MacArthur Foundation. Special gratitude to my editor, Paul Slovak, for more than twenty years of faith and support. Thanks as well to writers and artists who influenced this manuscript through encouragement and conversation: Elizabeth Alexander, Radiclani Clytus, Toi Derricotte, Joel Dias-Porter, Peter Kahn, Mary Karr, Virginia Jackson, Nick Laird, Shara McCallum, Jeffrey McDaniel, Ed Pavlic, Roger Reeves, and Joan Wasser. Special shouts to friends: the late David Berman, the late Lucie Brock-Broido, the late Wanda Coleman, and the late Tony Hoagland. I could not have completed this book without a lifetime of teachers. Special shouts to my parents and family.

HIP LOGIC

Terrance Hayes is a dazzlingly original poet, interested in adventurous explorations of subject and form. *Hip Logic* is full of poetic tributes to the likes of Paul Robeson, Big Bird, Balthus, and Mr. T, as well as poems based on the anagram principle of words within a word. Throughout, Hayes's verse dances in a kind of homemade music box, with notes that range from tender to erudite, associative to narrative, humorous to political.

WIND IN A BOX

Terrance Hayes is an elegant and adventurous writer with disarming humor, grace, tenderness, and brilliant turns of phrase. In this resonant collection, *Wind in a Box*, Hayes continues his interest in how traditions (of poetry and culture alike) can be simultaneously upended and embraced. The struggle for freedom (the wind) within containment (the box) is the unifying motif as Hayes explores how identity is shaped by race, heritage, and spirituality.

LIGHTHEAD

In his fourth collection, Terrance Hayes investigates how we construct experience. With one foot firmly grounded in the everyday and the other hovering in the air, his poems braid dream and reality into a poetry that is both dark and buoyant. This innovative collection, winner of the National Book Award, presents the lightheadedness of a mind trying to pull against gravity and time. Fueled by an imagination that delights, enlightens, and ignites, *Lighthead* leaves us illuminated and scorched.

PENGUIN BOOKS

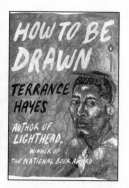

HOW TO BE DRAWN

In *How to Be Drawn*, Terrance Hayes explores how we see and are seen. While many of these poems bear the clearest imprint yet of Hayes's background as a visual artist, they do not strive to describe art so much as inhabit it. The formal and emotional versatilities that distinguish Hayes's award-winning poetry are unified by existential focus. Simultaneously complex and transparent, urgent and composed, *How to Be Drawn* is a mesmerizing achievement.

AMERICAN SONNETS FOR MY PAST AND FUTURE ASSASSIN

In seventy poems bearing the same title, Terrance Hayes explores the meanings of American, of assassin, and of love in the sonnet form. Written during the first two hundred days of the Trump presidency, these poems are haunted by the country's past and future eras and errors, its dreams and nightmares. The wonders of this collection are irreducible and stunning.

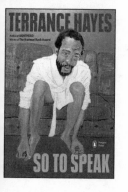

SO TO SPEAK

The three sections of this seventh collection explore how we see ourselves and our world, mapping the strange and lyrical grammar of thinking and feeling. In "Watch Your Mouth," a tree frog sings to overcome its fear of birds; in "Watch Your Step: The Kafka Virus," a talking cat tells jokes in the Jim Crow South; in "Watch Your Head," green beans bling in the mouth of Lil Wayne. *So to Speak* is the restless, mature work of one of contemporary poetry's leading voices.

🐧 PENGUIN BOOKS